Today's Homeowner®

Weekend Projects

80 EASY WAYS
TO IMPROVE
YOUR HOME

CREATIVE
PUBLISHING
international

Credits

Copyright © 1999 Creative Publishing
international, Inc., and Times Mirror Magazines, Inc.

Creative Publishing international, Inc.
5900 Green Oak Drive
Minnetonka, MN 55343
1-800-328-3895

TODAY'S HOMEOWNER is a registered trademark of
Times Mirror Magazines, Inc., and is used under license.

President: Iain Macfarlane
Director, Creative Development: Lisa Rosenthal
Executive Managing Editor: Elaine Perry

Executive Editor: Bryan Trandem
Associate Creative Director: Tim Himsel
Managing Editor: Jennifer Caliandro
Project Manager: Jill Anderson
Lead Editor: Rose Brandt
Senior Editor: Jerri Farris
Editors: Betty Christiansen, Phil Schmidt
Copy Editor: Janice Cauley
Senior Art Director: Kevin Walton
Mac Design Manager: Jon Simpson
Mac Designers: Patricia Goar, Brad Webster
Photo Researcher: Angie Spann
Illustrator: Richard Stromwell
Manager, Production Services: Kim Gerber
Production Manager: Stasia Dorn
Production Staff: Patrick Gibson, Laura Hokkanen

Today's Homeowner.

VP/Editor-in-Chief: Paul Spring
Executive Editor: Fran J. Donegan
Managing Editor: Steven H. Saltzman
Associate Art Director: Nancy Stamatopoulos
Senior Editors: Leslie Plummer Clagett, Lynn Ocone,
   Joseph Truini, John D. Wagner
Primary editor for *Weekend Projects:* Joseph Truini
Editorial Assistant: Victoria Egelbaum

VP/Publisher: John W. Young
General Manager: Jill Raufman
President, Today's Homeowner: Jason E. Klein

Library of Congress
Cataloging-in-Publication Data

Weekend projects : 80 easy ways to improve your home.
   p.   cm.
   At head of title: Today's homeowner.
   Includes index.
   ISBN 0-86573-778-9 (hc.). -- ISBN 0-86573-779-7 (softcover)
   1. Dwellings--Maintenance and repair Amateurs' manuals.
2. Dwellings--Remodeling Amateurs' manuals. 3. Interior decoration
Amateurs' manuals. I. Creative Publishing International.
II. Today's homeowner.
TH4817.3.W425 1999
643'.7--dc21   99-33032

Contents

Sprucing Up Walls   6

Texture Painting 8
Decorative Painting 10
Wallpaper Borders 12
Upholstered Walls 14
Wall Frame Molding 16
Crown Molding 18
Pressed-Metal Wainscoting 20
Library Panels 21
Designing with Mirrors 22
Mirrored Bath Ideas 24
Jewel Box Bath 26
Mirrored Backsplash 27

Upgrading Floors & Ceilings   30

Ceramic Tile Flooring 32
Vinyl Tile Flooring 34
Sheet Vinyl Flooring 36
Laminate Flooring 38
Layered Ceiling 42
Textured Ceiling 44
Embossed Tin Ceiling 45
Beadboard Ceiling 46

Making Baths Work Better   50

Porcelain Soap Dish 52
Slide-Bar Showerhead 53
Shower Seat 54
Glass Tub Enclosure 56
Solid-Surface Tub Surround 58

Lighting Up Your Home   62

Dimmer Switches 64
Specialty Switches 65
Recessed Lighting 66
Ceiling Fan-Light 68
Weatherizing Windows 70
Replacing Sashes 72
Interior Shutters 74
Glass Block Window 76
Tubular Skylight 80

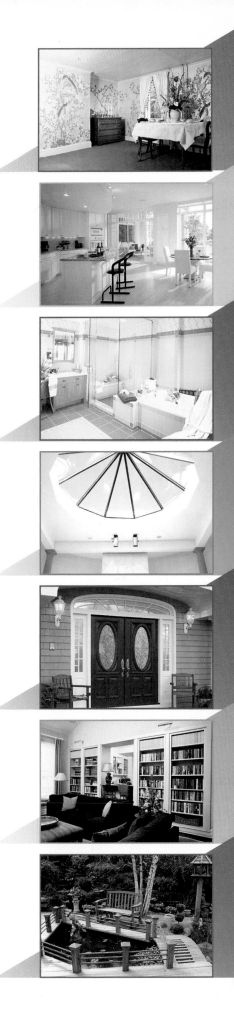

Renewing Doors & Entries   **84**

Weatherizing Doors *86*
Security Lock *88*
Securing a Door *89*
Grand Entrance *90*
Storm Door *94*
Classic Screen Door *96*
Bifold Closet Doors *98*

Adding Shelving & Storage   **102**

Mantel Shelf *104*
Bin-&-Shelving Units *106*
Wall Boxes *108*
Picture Frame Shelves *110*
Kitchen Wine Rack *112*
Stairway Pantry *114*
Wall-to-Wall Bookcases *116*
Entertainment Center *118*
Floor-to-Ceiling Shelves *122*
Lighting a Wall Unit *126*
Glide-Out Shelves *128*

Improving Your Yard   **132**

Stepping-Stone Path *134*
Outdoor Lighting *136*
Garden Pond *138*
Eastern Influence *142*
Cedar Louvers *143*
Tiered Planters *144*
Privacy Screen *145*
Cozy Corner *146*
Crossrail Classic *148*
Redwood Slats *149*
Patio Arbor *150*
Cedar Settee *154*

Index *157*

Sprucing Up Walls

❧

Add new style and
personality to drab,
ordinary walls
with paint, wallpaper,
molding and mirrors.

❧

Sprucing Up Walls

QUICK REFERENCE

WALL TREATMENTS	Texture Painting	page 8
	Decorative Painting	page 10
	Wallpaper Borders	page 12
	Upholstered Walls	page 14
WALL TRIM	Wall Frame Molding	page 16
	Crown Molding	page 18
WAINSCOTING	Pressed-Metal Wainscoting	page 20
	Library Panels	page 21
MIRRORS	Designing with Mirrors	page 22
	Mirrored Bath Ideas	page 24
	Jewel Box Bath	page 26
	Mirrored Backsplash	page 27

Although the walls of our homes are backdrops for all our indoor activities, too often we simply paint them white and maybe put up a picture or two. So it's easy to overlook the potential that a relatively simple wall improvement may have to significantly enhance a room's style, function and livability.

In this chapter, we'll look at a variety of simple ways to add interest to walls by using decorative painting and wallpapering techniques, wall trim and mirrors. The projects in this chapter require only simple do-it-yourself skills.

Wall Treatments

There are many excellent books that describe basic paint and wall-covering techniques; this section focuses specifically on decorative techniques that can add a creative finishing touch to your walls. They include texture painting, decorative painting, wallpaper borders and upholstered walls.

If you're new to painting or wallpapering, start small until you gain confidence and master the basic techniques involved.

Wall Trim

Another relatively easy way to add personality to a dull wall is to install trim, such as a wall frame molding, crown molding or wainscoting. All these wall trim projects require only basic carpentry skills.

Wall frame molding is very simple to install and offers an excellent design solution for a large expanse of unadorned wall.

Although crown molding can add great character to a room, traditional installation techniques require you to cut tricky compound and angled joints. The project shown here presents a much simpler approach.

Wainscoting

Wainscoting is a covering over the lower part of a wall that has both decorative and practical uses. In addition to adding the warmth of natural wood to a room, it helps protect the wall from wear and tear. Wainscoting is traditionally used in kitchens, baths, dining rooms, libraries and hallways.

Here we show you two easy and inexpensive styles: pressed-metal wainscoting (the embossed squares used for tin ceilings) and prefabricated oak veneer library panels. Either of these wainscotings can be installed in a medium-size room in a weekend.

Mirrors

Mirrors are perhaps the best way to create the illusion of space in a small or cramped room—and compared to other wall options, they're inexpensive and easy to install. Here you'll learn how to select and place mirrors to create the effect you're looking for, and how to mount and clean a mirror properly.

This section also offers several suggestions for using mirrors in a bathroom or kitchen. In many homes, the bathroom and kitchen are the smallest rooms—which means they have the most to gain from the space-expanding effect of a well-placed mirror.

TEXTURE PAINTING

Tools
- power drill with paint mixer
- tools to create texture: whisk broom, trowel, sponge, long-nap paint roller, paintbrush, etc.

Materials
- premixed latex texture paint or dry powder texture paint

Although texture is an important element of our homes, we often overlook the subtle background surfaces that surround us. Texture painting is a way to bring that element to the fore by adding a third dimension to walls.

The possibilities for texture painting variations are almost limitless. The depth of the texture you'll get will depend on the stiffness of the paint, the amount you apply to the surface and the tool you use to create the texture pattern.

As with any painting project, begin by washing and drying the walls thoroughly, to ensure that the paint will adhere properly to the surface. For best results, experiment with different textures on sheets of cardboard until you get the effect you're looking for.

Use a small whisk broom to create a swirl pattern.

Pile up thick paint with a trowel to create an adobe pattern.

Texture Painting Suggestions

Texture painting involves working thickened paint into an interesting pattern that adds a three-dimensional effect to a wall. You can use specially designed texture paint or powder and almost any kind of tool or instrument to create a textured effect.

Use a premixed latex texture paint to produce light stipple patterns, and a thicker powder texture to create heavier adobe or stucco finishes. To mix the powder texture with water, use a power drill fitted with a paint mixer attachment.

Here are some ideas for texture painting techniques to help you get started.

Stipple Texture

Use a long-nap roller. For different patterns, vary the pressure on the roller and the amount of texture paint on the surface of the wall.

Swirl Pattern

Apply the texture paint with a roller, then use a small whisk broom to create a repeated swirl design.

Adobe Pattern

Trowel texture material onto the surface and pile it up in ridges.

Brocade Design

Trowel over the partially dried paint to flatten the peaks. Clean the trowel after each stroke with a wet brush or sponge.

Stucco Pattern

Dab, drag or swirl a sponge over texture paint until you find a texture you like.

Two-Tone Stucco

Sponge on a layer of texture paint. Let the paint dry, then sponge another color over it.

Crowsfoot Design

Apply texture paint with a roller. Brush it level, then randomly strike the surface with the flat of a brush.

Stomp Design

Randomly press the flat side of a trowel into the texture paint, then pull it away.

Use a long-nap paint roller to create a stipple effect.

For a crowsfoot look, strike the wall with the side of a brush.

DECORATIVE PAINTING

Sponging. Press the sponge gently onto the wall with a quick, light touch. Allow the first accent color to dry before adding the next one.

Decorative painting techniques offer an easy and inexpensive way to add visual texture to walls. All you need is a sponge, some paint and a clean, dry wall.

For a watercolor effect, use soft, light colors. For a bolder look, select colors with strong contrasts. Often, the second-darkest color is used as the base coat, and the accent colors are applied from darkest to lightest.

You can use the techniques shown here either together or separately. Before you start, experiment on cardboard to see the effect you'll get.

Sponging

A. Apply a base coat of the desired background color to a clean, prepared surface. Allow to dry.

B. Rinse a natural sea sponge in water to soften it; squeeze it dry.

C. Pour a little of the first accent color onto a paint tray. Dab the sponge in the paint, taking care not to overload it. Blot it on newsprint until it makes a light impression.

D. Using a quick, light touch, press the sponge gently onto the wall (don't drag it). Turn it often to produce an irregular effect. (If you'll be adding another color, apply the first color sparingly.)

E. Apply the first color to the entire area, until the individual sponge marks are no longer obvious. Stand back often to examine the wall, and fill in as necessary.

Tools
- natural sea sponge
- paint tray
- newsprint or scrap paper
- veining feather or fine fan brush
- paintbrush

Materials
- 1 quart low-luster latex enamel interior paint per color
- metallic paint (for veining)

F. Allow the first color to dry. Rinse the sponge and the paint tray.

G. Repeat these steps for each color of paint. When you apply the last color, fill in between the earlier sponge marks, to blend the colors.

Marbling

A. Following the instructions for Sponging, apply the first accent paint in diagonal drifts that meander randomly up the wall.

B. Soften the edges of the drifts by gently blotting wet paint with a tissue and lightly whisking a dry paintbrush over the surface.

C. Apply the second color of paint or glaze in a lighter tone, blending the textures and colors.

D. Embellish the surface by veining it (see below).

Veining

A. Select a metallic paint or an accent color. If you'd like a translucent effect, thin the paint with water.

B. Dip the tip of a turkey quill feather or fine fan brush into the paint. (Veining feathers are available in the paint department of home improvement stores.) Remove excess paint on a piece of newsprint.

C. Draw the tip of the feather or brush lightly along the surface at a 45-degree angle. Use a trembling motion so the veins wave, break off and reappear. Fork the veins, and cross one over another.

D. When crossing over a vein, lift the feather or brush and shift direction.

E. To vary the width of a vein, twist your wrist as you move the feather along.

Marbling. After sponging on the first color in diagonal drifts, apply a lighter color of paint or glaze over it.

Veining. Using a trembling motion, draw the tip of a feather or a fan brush lightly over the prepared surface.

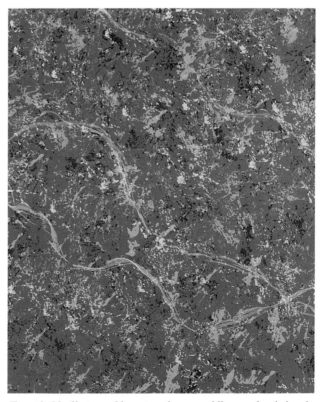

For a bold effect, combine sponging, marbling and veining in high-contrast colors with metallic paint highlights.

WALLPAPER BORDERS

Border strips made of wallcovering materials are a unique way to add style to a room or to highlight an architectural feature, such as a fireplace mantel. You can use these borders in any room and on both painted and wallpapered surfaces.

Interesting borders are easy to find or make. Matching borders are available for many wallcovering designs (check the sample books in a wallpaper store). You can also create your own customized borders by cutting full-size wallpaper into narrow strips. To make this job easier, use a striped pattern with a nondirectional design. For another interesting effect, trim around the outline of a pattern inside a wide stripe.

There are many possible ways to place a wallpaper border in a room. Use it as a crown molding around the perimeter of a ceiling. Position the border so that it frames a window, door or fireplace. On a painted wall, create a chair rail border or place a line of wallpaper along the top of the wainscoting.

Tools
- ruler
- level
- sharp utility knife
- wide broadknife
- straightedge
- smoothing brush
- seam roller
- sponge

Materials
- wallcovering border
- wallcovering paste
- seam adhesive

Step 1

A. Plan the layout of the border, starting in the least conspicuous corner of the room.

B. If the border isn't being placed along a ceiling or baseboard, draw a light pencil line around the wall at the desired height, using a level as a guide. Measure the line down from the ceiling or up from the floor, whichever is shorter.

Step 2

A. Cut and prepare the first border strip.

B. Beginning at the selected corner, apply the border along the reference line, overlapping it onto the adjacent wall by ½ in.

C. Press the border flat along the wall with a smoothing brush. Have a helper unfold the unused portion of the border as you apply and brush it into place.

Step 2

Begin by overlapping the border ½ in. around the first corner. Press it down with a smoothing brush.

Step 3

Form a ¼-in. tuck just beyond the inside corner, then continue applying the border and cut it at the corner.

Step 3

A. Form a ¼-in. tuck just beyond each inside corner, then continue to apply the border.

B. Cut the border at the corner using a utility knife and broadknife.

C. Peel back the tucked strip and smooth it around the corner. Press the border flat.

D. Apply seam adhesive to the lapped seam, if necessary.

Step 4

A. For seams that fall in the middle of a wall, overlap the border strips so the patterns match.

B. Cut through both layers with a utility knife, then peel back the border and remove the cut ends.

C. Press the border flat. After half an hour, roll the seam.

D. Rinse excess adhesive from the border, using a damp sponge.

Step 5

A. To cut-in the border flush with wallcovering, overlap the border onto the wallcovering.

B. Use a straightedge and a utility knife to cut through the underlying wallcovering along the border edge.

C. Pull up the border; remove excess wallcovering. Press the border down flat.

HOW TO MITER BORDER CORNERS

Step 1

A. Apply the horizontal border strip first. Extend it past the corner farther than the width of the border.

B. Apply the vertical border strip the same way, overlapping the horizontal strip.

C. Check the strips to make sure the pattern will meet at the diagonal cut. If necessary, adjust the position of the strips.

Step 2

A. Cut through both layers of border at a 45-degree angle, using a utility knife and a straightedge.

B. Peel back the end of the border; remove both cut sections.

C. Press the border flat. Wait half an hour, then roll the seam.

D. Wipe any remaining adhesive from the seam with a damp sponge.

Cut through both layers of border at a 45-degree angle. Peel the border back, remove the cut pieces and press flat.

UPHOLSTERED WALLS

Step 1

A. Buy and cut the fabric, welting and batting (see fabric worksheet). Don't trim the selvages unless they show through the fabric.

B. Measure around doors and windows and along the ceiling and baseboard. Measure from the floor to the ceiling at each corner.

C. Cut 3-in.-wide fabric strips, equal to the total of these measurements, for the double welting.

Step 2

A. Remove switch plates and outlet covers from the walls. Don't remove moldings or baseboards—the double welting will cover the fabric edges.

B. Staple batting to the wall every 6 in., leaving a 1-in. gap between the batting and the edge of the ceiling, corners, baseboard and moldings.

C. Butt the edges between widths of batting and cut the batting to fit around switch and outlet openings.

Step 3

A. Stitch the fabric panels together for each wall separately, matching the pattern. Avoid placing seams next to windows and doors.

B. Beginning at an inconspicuous corner, hang the fabric from the top,

Upholstering walls with decorator fabric offers practical benefits as well as a striking, elegant appearance. The fabric covers any imperfections in the wall surface, and its padding insulates the room and absorbs sound.

However, there are a few things to watch out for. Avoid fabrics with plaids or stripes; they'll call attention to walls that aren't square. It's easy to staple fabric to paneling, but drywall requires a little more planning. Staples won't penetrate the metal corner bead used on outside corners, so you'll have to wrap the fabric around them. If you have plaster walls, make sure the staples will hold before you begin.

Step 3

Anchor fabric to the corners, pulling it taut and stapling it close to corners.

Step 5

Cut openings for doors and windows with diagonal cuts into the corners.

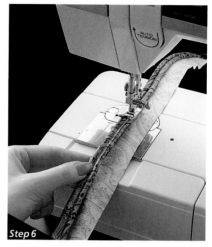

Step 6

To finish the double welting, stitch between the cords.

turning under ½ in. and stapling every 3 to 4 in. Don't cut around the windows and doors.

C. Anchor the fabric in the corners, pulling it taut and stapling close to the corner (the staples will be covered with double welting).

D. Trim the excess fabric and start the next panel at the next corner.

Step 4

A. Staple along the baseboard, pulling and smoothing the fabric taut to remove any wrinkles.

B. Use a single-edged razor blade to trim the excess fabric along the baseboard.

Step 5

A. Mark the outside corners of the windows and doors with pushpins. Cut out openings with diagonal cuts into the corners.

B. Turn under the raw edges and staple around the molding.

Step 6

A. Make the double welting by placing cording on the wrong side of a 3-in.-wide fabric strip. Fold the fabric over the cording with a ½-in. seam allowance extending. Use a

zipper foot to stitch next to the cording.

B. Place the second cord next to the first. Bring the fabric over the second length of cording.

C. Stitch between the two cords on the previous stitching line. Trim off excess fabric next to the stitching; the raw edge is on the back of finished double welting.

Step 7

A. Apply hot glue to the back of the double welting, about 5 in. at a time. Secure the double welting to the upper and lower edges of the wall and around window and door frames, covering the staples.

B. Press the double welting into the corners and around any openings, using a screwdriver to push it into the corners. After the glue dries, peel off any excess.

Step 8

A. Apply fabric to the switch plates and outlet covers, securing it with diluted craft glue.

B. Clip and trim the fabric around the openings. Turn the raw edges to the back of the plate and glue them in place.

Fabric Worksheet

Cut Length	**in.**
Measurement from floor to ceiling, plus 3 in.*	= _____
Cut Width	
Width of fabric minus selvages	= _____
Number of Fabric Widths Needed	
for Each Wall	
Width of wall	= _____
Divided by cut width of fabric	/ _____
Number of fabric widths for wall**	= _____
Amount of Fabric Needed	
for Double Welting	
Total welting length (see Step 1)	= _____
Divided by cut width of fabric	/ _____
Number of strips**	= _____
Multiplied by 3 in.	x 3
Fabric needed for double welting	= _____
Total Fabric Needed	
Cut length (figured above)	= _____
Number of fabric widths (figured above) for all walls	x _____
Fabric needed for all walls	= _____
Fabric needed for double welting	+ _____
Total length needed	= _____
Divided by 36 in.	/ 36
Number of yds. needed	= _____

*Allow extra for pattern repeat; don't subtract for windows and doors unless they cover most of the wall.

**Round up to the nearest whole number.

WALL FRAME MOLDING

Wall frame moldings are an elegant way to add a distinctive touch to a wall. They can accent special features, divide large walls into smaller sections or add interest to an otherwise plain surface.

The molding can be single or double, the same color as the walls or a contrasting shade. You can highlight the frames by wallpapering the area within the frame or painting it a different color than the surrounding wall.

To plan the size and location of the frames, cut paper strips the width of the moldings and experiment by taping them to the wall. Try to repeat the shape, size or visual line of other design elements in the room, such as the windows or a fireplace mantel.

Install the molding with small finishing nails placed near the outside corners of the molding and through the wall studs (use nails long enough to go through the wall and into the studs). If the vertical pieces aren't placed over a wall stud, apply wood glue to the back of the molding pieces to keep them from pulling away from the wall.

Add interest to an otherwise plain wall by covering the framed area with wallpaper.

Tools	Materials
• level	• paper
• backsaw & miter box or power miter saw	• tape
	• decorative molding
	• wood glue
• drill with 1/16-in. bit	• paint or stain
• carpenter's square	• putty to match paint or stain
• nailset	• finishing nails

Cut paper strips in the form of the molding and tape them to the wall. Mark the upper corners with a pencil.

Nail the upper molding strip to the wall, aligning it with the pencil marks.

Step 1

A. Cut paper strips the width and length of the molding.

B. Tape the strips to the wall exactly as you want to position the wall moldings, making sure the upper strip is level.

C. Lightly mark the outer corners of the upper strip with a pencil.

Step 2

A. Measure the molding and mark the miters on the top and bottom molding pieces.

B. Cut the ends of the molding at opposite 45-degree angles, using a backsaw and a miter box or a power miter saw. The two pieces must be exactly the same length.

C. Repeat steps 2A and 2B for the side strips.

D. Paint or stain the moldings as desired. Predrill nail holes near the ends of all the molding pieces.

Step 3

A. Position the top molding piece on the wall, aligning it with the pencil marks.

B. If the molding won't be nailed into wall studs, place dots of glue sparingly on the back.

C. Nail the molding to the wall, leaving the nails slightly raised.

Step 4

A. Position the side frame molding pieces on the wall, making sure they're square. Nail the upper corners only.

B. Position the lower piece on the wall, making sure it's square and level. Nail it to the wall.

C. Drive the remaining nails into the side frame pieces.

Step 5

A. Using the nailset and a hammer, tap the nails slightly below the surface of the frame.

B. Touch up the nail holes and the mitered corners using wood putty and paint, or tinted wood putty.

Check to make sure that the corners are square, then nail the molding in place.

CROWN MOLDING

Crown molding is a powerful architectural accent that can dramatically change the look of a room without overpowering other elements. While it has graced cottages and castles alike for centuries, it's less common in modern homes, because installing it takes time and requires a highly skilled carpenter.

Traditionally, crown molding has been nailed to the wall and the ceiling at an angle—which involves cutting a tricky compound-angle miter joint where the molding turns an outside corner. Inside corners are traditionally just as difficult, requiring another compound-angle joint or a coped cut. These are all fussy joints to fit, and mistakes are expensive.

However, there's now a fast, foolproof way to add the classic beauty of crown molding to your home—and it doesn't require making a single angle cut.

The beautiful dentil crown molding shown here looks as if it's made of solid mahogany, but it's actually molded from lightweight, high-density urethane foam. It features premolded corner blocks, which eliminate the need to cut angled joints. You simply nail up the corner blocks and square-cut the molding to fit between them. In addition to the corner blocks, there are also divider blocks that simplify joining two lengths of molding along a long wall.

Hundreds of urethane molding styles are available in both 8- and 12-ft. lengths. Most are available in both a stainable wood-grain finish and a paint-grade white finish that resembles traditional plaster moldings.

See **Grand Entrance**, pages 90-93, for another way to use urethane millwork to add the elegance of classic wood trim to your home.

Tools
- hammer
- power miter saw, radial arm saw, or fine-tooth handsaw
- nailset
- 1-in. paintbrush

Materials
- molded urethane molding, corner blocks & divider blocks (if needed)
- paint or stain
- 2-in. (6d) finishing nails
- caulk to match the molding
- crayon-type putty stick to match the molding

Step 1

Before installing all the moldings and accessories, you need to paint or stain them to match the existing wood trim.

Painting: No primer is needed; the moldings are preprimed and will accept any good-quality latex or oil-based paint.

Staining: Use a thick-bodied gel stain or a controlled-penetration stain. Don't use a semitransparent stain; it's too thin to tint the nonporous urethane.

Apply the paint or stain with a 1-in.-wide paintbrush, taking care to fully cover the dentil detailing.

Step 2

A. Nail up all the inside corner blocks. If the wall corners are out of square (as most are), slip a few narrow shims behind the blocks to fill the gaps.

B. Nail up any outside corner blocks in the same way.

C. If you need to put up two lengths of molding to complete a long wall, center a divider block between them.

Outside corner blocks eliminate the need to cut compound angles in the molding. Secure them with nails.

Step 3

A. Carefully measure the distance between one pair of corner blocks.

B. Add ⅛ in. to that dimension and cut a length of crown molding to match.

The most accurate way to crosscut the molding is with a power miter saw or a radial arm saw, but you can also get excellent results with a fine-tooth handsaw. To get a square cut, clamp a short 1×4 to the molding and use it as a saw guide.

Step 4

A. Hold the molding in place and butt one end tightly against a corner block. Bow it slightly and insert the other end in the other corner block. Press the molding to the wall until it pops into place. Secure it with 6d finishing nails driven into every other wall stud.

B. Drive a nail up into a ceiling joist every few feet. (If you can't find the ceiling joists, they may be running parallel to the molding. In that case, angle a nail up into the drywall or the plaster ceiling.)

Step 5

Continue cutting and installing the molding to fit between the corner (and divider) blocks. If you cut a piece slightly too short, fill the gap with a matching caulk. Also fill any gaps along the wall or ceiling.

Step 6

When all the molding is up, set the nailheads and fill the holes with a crayon-type putty stick. Remove any excess putty with a damp cloth.

Nail up the inside corner blocks, after shimming them as needed.

Raise the molding into position and pop it into place between the corner blocks. Continue until all the molding is installed, then caulk any gaps.

PRESSED-METAL WAINSCOTING

Embossed pressed-metal sheets are actually reproductions of the old tin plates used on ceilings. They're affordable and available in many styles and sizes.

All you need to install them are a few hand tools and a good pair of tin snips. However, since the edges are very sharp, always wear leather work gloves when you handle them.

To provide support for nailing the metal sheets, screw furring strips to the wall.

Step 2

Step 1

Paint the back of each metal sheet with an oil-based primer to protect against rusting.

Step 2

Secure 1×3 furring strips to the wall with screws.

Space the horizontal strips to provide a nailing base for the top, middle and bottom of the pressed-metal sheets, the chair rail and the baseboard molding.

Space the vertical strips 24 in. on center, to align with the ends and middle of the metal sheets.

Step 3

Install the baseboard molding.

Step 4

Starting in the most visible corner of the room, attach the metal sheets to the furring strips, using the decorative cone-head nails that come with them. When you get to a corner, use the tin snips to cut the panels to fit.

Step 5

Install the chair rail. Refer to the diagram at right for a simple chair rail made from two pieces of pine and base cap molding.

3/4" x 13/4" shop-made rail cap

3/8" x 13/4" pine

1x3

11/8" base cap molding

24"-high x 48"-long metal panel

1x3

11/8" base cap molding

1x3 ripped to fit

1x4

1x3

Shoe molding

Tools
- paintbrush
- tin snips
- hammer
- leather work gloves
- screwdriver

Materials
- pressed-metal sheets, with decorative cone-head nails
- oil-based primer
- 1x3 furring strips
- chair rail
- baseboard molding
- screws

LIBRARY PANELS

Prefabricated frame-and-panel wainscoting can evoke the traditional look of cherry, mahogany, walnut or oak library panels—but is far easier to install.

The design shown mimics the look of red oak. The sheets are 30 in. high × 48 in. wide, and divided into three recessed panels. The frame is made of red oak-veneer fiberboard bonded to an oak plywood backboard. The exposed edges of the fiberboard frame are trimmed with a decorative solid-oak molding.

Fasten the wainscoting panels with drywall screws. Install a plywood strip to support the baseboard molding.

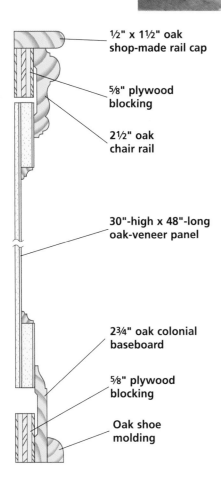

½" x 1½" oak shop-made rail cap

⅝" plywood blocking

2½" oak chair rail

30"-high x 48"-long oak-veneer panel

2¾" oak colonial baseboard

⅝" plywood blocking

Oak shoe molding

Step 1
Plan the layout of the panels from the most visible corner of the room outward. Ideally, electrical outlets will be centered in a frame. (You may want to have an electrician move outlets before you install the wainscoting.)

Step 2
Fasten the panels into place with drywall screws driven into wall studs. Drive the screws along the top and bottom edges of the panels so they'll be concealed by the chair rail and baseboard moldings. Butt the edges of the panels together to form a tight joint.

Step 3
Install strips of ⅝-in. plywood to provide a nailing base for the chair rail and baseboard moldings.

Step 4
Nail the chair rail and baseboard moldings to the plywood strips.

Step 5
If the panels are unfinished, apply two coats of varnish. You can stain them first, if you wish.

Materials
- prefabricated wood-veneer frame-and-panel sheets
- drywall screws
- ⅝-in. plywood strips
- chair rail
- baseboard molding
- stain (optional)
- varnish
- finishing nails

Tools
- screwdriver
- hammer

DESIGNING WITH MIRRORS

Mirrors can enhance almost any room—but the most effective type, size and location of the mirrors you choose will depend on the room's size and what you want to accomplish. Do you want to expand the space, multiply the light, add drama to the room—or all three?

To create the illusion of expanded space, use a few large floor-to-ceiling mirror panels and hide their seams (as shown above). Use an odd number of panels and avoid dividing the wall in the center. For example, on a 12-ft. wall, use three 4-ft. panels or one 6-ft. panel flanked by two 3-ft. panels.

To make a room look brighter, use large panels and be sure to reflect the light sources in the mirror. Consider using a lattice over the mirror—the mirror will reflect light, and the lattice will diffuse it. Don't

use smoked mirrors, which will make the room look darker.

If adding drama is your top priority, consider using several narrow strips applied to the walls or ceiling.

To avoid visual confusion, don't mirror more than two walls in one room. And finally, don't forget that the mirrors must be able to fit through all the doors that lead to the installation site.

Tools
- screwdriver
- drill

Materials
- ¼-in. mirror panels (from a glazier)
- mechanical mirror supports: screws, frames, clips, L-channel or J-channel
- mirror mastic

Using Mastic & Fasteners

Wall- and ceiling-mounted mirrors are held in place by mastic. Since mastic remains pliable even when fully cured, it's able to absorb vibrations in the mounting surface. However, be sure to use only mastic that's specifically labeled for mirrors; some adhesives, including silicone, contain solvents that will corrode the mirror backing.

Mirror mastic is available in both rubber- or asphalt-based formulas, as well as quick-setting varieties.

Asphalt-based mastic is the most common variety. If you're using it, the wall surface behind the mirror must be primed—untreated drywall or plywood will ruin the mastic. Asphalt-based mastic requires three to four days to cure. Use shims and double-stick tape to keep the mirror in place in the meantime.

This multipanel mirror reflects an outside view, creating a sense of endless space.

Step 1

Install the mechanical supports for the lower edge of the mirror, making sure that they're level.

Step 2

Cover the back of the mirror with mastic, spacing dabs about the size of a chocolate kiss about 8 in. apart.

If the wall behind the mirror isn't plumb, use a stiffer mastic, such as building mastic, which requires dabs about the size of Ping-Pong balls. The gap-filling capability of stiffer mastics makes them the best choice for walls that are irregular or slightly bowed.

Step 3

Slip the mirror into the bottom supports and then push it up against the wall.

Adjust it for position. If the bottom supports were carefully leveled, any adjustments should be minor.

Step 4

Install mechanical supports for the sides and top of the mirror, if necessary.

Rubber-based mastic forms a strong bond that's almost impossible to break. This can be a problem if you ever want to remove the mirror. Rubber-based mastic usually cures within six hours.

Quick-setting mastic sets up in about four hours. Some varieties are designed only for unprimed, porous substrates, while others are designed for nonporous surfaces, such as tile. Check the label to be sure you get the type you need.

Although mirror mastic is strong, it's best to provide additional support along the bottom of large mirrors, especially if they will be subjected to a lot of movement (such as on the back of a door). Another option is to make a lip for a mirror by setting it into drywall or tile.

Install support hardware for the bottom edge before mounting the mirror. (The side or top supports can be added after the mirror is in place.) If you choose not to install any mechanical supports, use temporary supports (cardboard or wood shims) to hold the mirror in place until the mastic sets.

Mounting a Mirror

Actually, the hardest part of mounting a mirror isn't attaching it, but getting it straight. Here are the steps involved in mounting a mirror properly.

BUYING MIRRORS

Home centers sell precut, full-length mirrors that are ready to install on the back of a closet, bedroom or bathroom door. But if you want to mirror a wall or replace the broken mirror above your bath vanity, you'll need to find a local shop that specializes in cutting and installing mirror and glass.

In general, consider hiring a glazier if you're dealing with a mirror bigger than about 2×3 ft. Trying to transport, cut and mount anything much larger is risky and not really cost-effective.

Mirror stock comes in three thicknesses: ⅛ and ³/₁₆ in., which are both used in frames, and ¼ in., which can be attached to walls in large sections with mastic and mechanical fasteners.

The mirror stock from all sources is basically the same; it's the finishing and the installation that determine the final appearance and expense of a mirror.

MIRRORED BATH IDEAS

Mirrors are one of the best ways to create a feeling of spaciousness in a dark or cramped area—and perhaps nowhere is this illusion more effective than in bathrooms, which can be both dark and small. In addition, using plenty of mirrors in the bath means you won't have to vie with your spouse for the one over the vanity in the morning.

Avoid installing bathroom mirrors from the floor to the ceiling. Begin the mirror at waist height or above so it won't reflect the plumbing or the toilet.

Here are two creative ways to use reflective surfaces to brighten up a bathroom.

Glass Ceiling

This 5 × 8-ft. bathroom feels spacious because of the mirror panels that cover the ceiling.

In addition, placing mirrors at either side of the short wall over the vanity visually doubles the length of this wall. Ending the mirrors at the front edge of the vanity prevents you from seeing infinite reflected images of yourself every time you stand at the sink.

While mechanical fasteners are usually necessary to hold mirrors on ceilings, here a marble wall tile forms a ⅜-in. lip to support the mirror. The mirror panels are also glued to the ceiling with mastic.

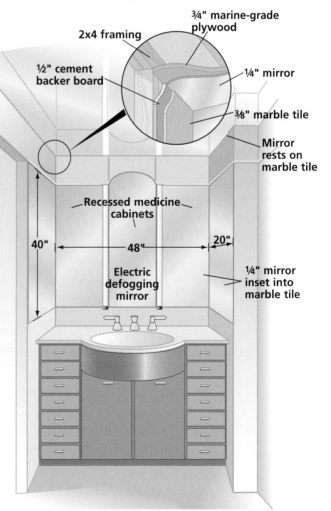

Tools
- screwdriver
- drill

Materials
- ¼-in. mirror panel (from a glazier)
- mechanical mirror supports: screws, frames, clips, L-channel or J-channel
- mirror mastic

Mirrored Sky

This cramped, windowless bath used to feel claustrophobic. But now a 1-ft. band of mirrors, combined with a trompe l'oeil overhead scene, make the low ceiling look as if it's floating in space—giving a bather an expansive skylike view.

The ⅜-in. tile and the ¼-in. mirrors are both laid over the same backer board, and the mirror seams are aligned to the tile grout lines. Since the mastic adds some thickness to the back of the mirror, the finished surfaces are flush, and the look is sleek and elegant.

THE RIGHT WAY TO CLEAN MIRRORS

Moisture is a mirror's number one enemy. When you spray wet glass cleaner onto a mirror, it can puddle in the seams and edges, invade the mirror's protective coating and eventually deteriorate its reflective surface. That's the cause of those ugly black spots on old mirrors.

Instead of spritzing glass cleaner onto the mirror, follow these suggestions:

• Use a lint-free paper towel or a clean, soft cotton cloth. Old diapers and T-shirts work great.

• Spray a nonabrasive, low-ammonia cleaner onto the cloth, not the mirror, so it won't seep into the seams.

• Another option is to moisten the cloth in 1 gal. of water mixed with 1 cup rubbing alcohol or ¾ cup distilled white vinegar.

• Finish the process by drying the mirror thoroughly with a soft, grit-free cloth, paying special attention to the seams and edges.

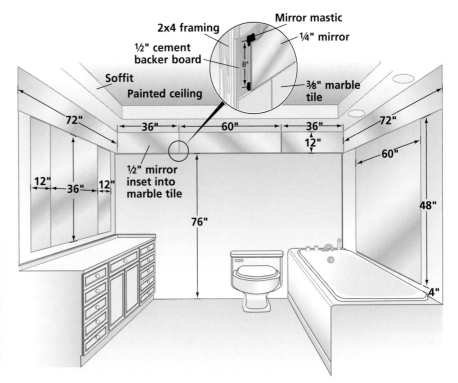

JEWEL BOX BATH

Measuring just 5 × 5½ ft., this windowless bathroom is hardly bigger than a modest walk-in closet. However, three mirrored and lighted niches have turned it into a bright, delightful retreat. The niches are lined with ¼-in. mirror panels and lighted with miniature halogen fixtures that are magnified by reflection. Here's how to create this look in your bathroom:

Step 1

A. Cut open three recessed niches in the wall between studs (usually they'll be 14½ in. wide × 4 in. deep).

B. Purchase small "hockey-puck" halogen light fixtures. Position them and determine where the wiring will run. Prepare the wiring for the fixtures in the wall.

C. Nail blocking between the studs to form the top and bottom of each niche. Drill a hole for the fixture wires through the blocking at the top of the niche.

D. Cut pieces of ¼-in. plywood to line the top, bottom, sides and back of the niches. Drill a hole for the fixture wires in the top piece. Glue the back piece in place, then nail or screw in the other pieces.

Step 2

Measure the wall niches carefully and figure the exact dimensions of the glass shelves and the top, bottom, side and back mirror panels. Design each side mirror panel in three sections, allowing for ¼-in. voids between the sections. Also mark a wiring hole in the top mirror panel, aligned with the one in the plywood. Order the glass and mirror from a glazier to fit your measurements.

Step 3

A. Use mastic to attach the mirror panels to the plywood, leaving ¼-in. grooves between the side sections to hold the glass shelves.

B. Place silicone adhesive in the grooves and install the glass shelves.

C. Frame the niches with metal edging.

D. Wire and install the lights at the top of each niche.

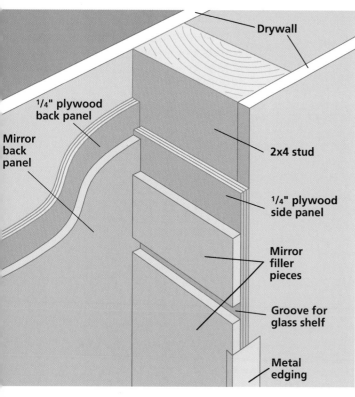

Drywall

¼" plywood back panel

Mirror back panel

2x4 stud

¼" plywood side panel

Mirror filler pieces

Groove for glass shelf

Metal edging

Tools
- wallboard saw
- utility knife
- hammer
- painting supplies
- paint
- ¼-in. mirror, custom-cut
- ¼-in. glass shelves
- mirror mastic
- silicone adhesive
- metal edging
- "hockey-puck" halogen fixtures, ¾-in. deep x 2½-in. dia.

Materials
- nails
- blocking pieces
- ¼-in. plywood

MIRRORED BACKSPLASH

This kitchen offers a striking combination of reflective surfaces: a mirrored and lighted backsplash set against black granite countertops.

Continuing the granite up the wall would have made the room look dark; the mirrored backsplash not only shows off the beauty of the countertops, but also reflects outdoor light and the light of the halogen fixtures under the upper cabinets. The mirrors actually double the brightness of the kitchen and make it appear larger.

Mirrors are inexpensive compared to other backsplash materials, such as stone and tile. They stand up well to heat, are easy to clean and are practically stainproof. Also, a mirrored backsplash allows you to keep an eye on activities elsewhere in the room while you cook.

The backsplash shown here was installed in three separate panels: two 15-in.-tall panels over the countertops and one 30-in.-tall panel over the stove. The mirrors were installed directly over the existing drywall surface.

For information on undercabinet lighting, see **Lighting a Wall Unit,** pages 126-127.

Step 1

A. Measure the mirror dimensions carefully, allowing for a ⅛-in. airspace between the bottom edge of the mirror and the countertop.

B. Order the mirrors from a glazier to fit your dimensions.

Step 2

A. Install J-channel on the wall along the base of the mirrors.

B. Insert neoprene-rubber setting blocks every 6 to 8 in. in the J-channel to lift the mirrors away from the moisture that may collect there. (This step isn't necessary for small mirrors if you can attach screw-in mirror holders to the wall.)

Step 3

A. Cover the back of the mirror with dollops of mirror mastic, spaced about 8 in. apart.

B. Position the mirrors and shim them into place until the mastic is fully cured.

Tools
- screwdriver

Materials
- ¼-in. mirror panels, custom-cut
- mirror mastic
- J-channel or screw-in mirror holders
- neoprene-rubber setting blocks

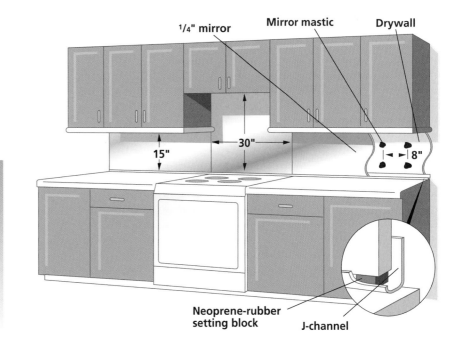

¼" mirror   Mirror mastic   Drywall

15"   30"   8"

Neoprene-rubber setting block   J-channel

Upgrading Floors & Ceilings

Give any room a dramatic new look with one of these surprisingly easy weekend makeovers.

*U*pgrading Floors & Ceilings

QUICK REFERENCE

FLOORS	*Ceramic Tile Flooring*	*page 32*
	Vinyl Tile Flooring	*page 34*
	Sheet Vinyl Flooring	*page 36*
	Laminate Flooring	*page 38*
CEILINGS	*Layered Ceiling*	*page 42*
	Textured Ceiling	*page 44*
	Embossed Tin Ceiling	*page 45*
	Beadboard Ceiling	*page 46*

Floors and ceilings offer many interesting ways to update a room at a relatively low cost. In this chapter you'll find out how easy it can be to transform a worn-out floor with splashes of color, eye-catching patterns or convincing facsimiles of stone, marble and premium hardwoods. You'll also discover how to add distinction to a ceiling with traditional beadboard, reproduction tin ceilings or the clean, modern lines of easy-to-install drywall panels.

Although the projects in this chapter require some specialized skills, if you start with a small area and follow the instructions carefully, you'll be able to learn them as you go along. In addition, all of these projects will go easier (and faster) with two people.

Flooring

This section describes how to install four kinds of flooring—ceramic tile, resilient vinyl tile, resilient sheet vinyl and laminate. In general, all these floors can be installed over any smooth, sound surface and can transform a small room in one weekend.

A ceramic tile bathroom floor is a project that even a beginner can accomplish in a few days. It's relatively inexpensive and will result in an elegant, durable and watertight floor.

Vinyl tile is a good choice for any room where moisture isn't likely to be a factor. For a high-moisture area such as a bathroom or laundry room, choose sheet vinyl instead.

Laminate flooring is increasingly popular, due to its durability and ability to mimic more expensive flooring materials. Like the other flooring projects shown here, the difficulty of the task will depend largely on the size of the room and the complexity of the cuts involved.

The key to a successful flooring installation is planning ahead, making sure you have the right equipment and following the directions carefully. Taking shortcuts, especially in the preparation phase, can lead to problems later.

Ceilings

Although ceilings are the most visible single surface in a room, most are simply painted white and then ignored (unless they spring a leak). However, there are several easy-to-install materials that can help you turn a blank, boring ceiling into the focal point of a room.

Drywall panels are a modern way to add style to a ceiling and define the boundaries of a living area. They're especially effective when used in "open" home designs as a way to break up a large expanse of ceiling.

Beadboard and embossed metal panels are popular ceiling coverings that can provide a room with a warm, traditional look and feel. Here we show you how easy they can be to install yourself.

CERAMIC TILE FLOORING

When remodeling a bathroom, glazed ceramic tile is often the flooring of choice—it's durable, attractive, easy to clean, water-resistant, affordable and easy to install.

You can lay new ceramic tile right over an existing ceramic tile floor (as shown here), as long as the surface is sound and doesn't flex when you walk on it. However, if the existing flooring is rotted, or if more than 10 percent of the old tiles are loose, you will need to remove them all and level the floor.

Step 1

A. Check the existing floor for stability. Repair or reinforce the floor and subfloor, if necessary.

B. If the tile will be laid over existing tiles, pound them with a rubber mallet to detect any loose tiles. If you find any, remove them, apply tile adhesive and glue them back down.

C. Clean the floor thoroughly.

Step 2

A. Draw layout lines on the floor, as described in steps 1 and 2 of **Vinyl Tile Flooring**, pages 34-35.

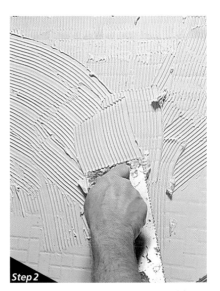

Spread thinset mortar onto the old floor with a notched trowel.

Tools
- tape measure
- chalkline
- ⅛-in. notched trowel
- rubber mallet
- 2x4 board
- handheld tile cutter
- tile nippers
- wet saw with diamond blade or jigsaw with tungsten-carbide blade
- circular saw with masonry abrasive blade
- needlenose pliers
- rubber grout float
- grout sponge
- soft cloth
- small brush or sponge

Materials
- glazed tile
- plastic tile spacers
- epoxy-based thin-set mortar
- marble threshold
- grout
- grout sealer

B. Starting in the center of the room, spread epoxy-based thinset mortar evenly against both reference lines of one quadrant, using a ⅛-in. notched trowel. Don't spread mortar over more than 2 sq. ft. at once; it will dry out before you're done.

Step 3

A. Set the first tile in the corner of the quadrant where the reference lines intersect. Press the tile into the adhesive with a slight twisting motion.

B. Ensure consistent spacing between tiles by placing plastic tile spacers at the corners of the set tile.

C. Position and set adjacent tiles into the adhesive along the reference lines. Make sure the tiles fit neatly against the spacers.

D. After setting several adjacent tiles, lay a straight 2×4 across them. Rap the 2×4 with a rubber mallet to ensure tiles are level with each other. Repeat this as you continue to lay the tile.

E. Lay the tiles in the remaining area of the quadrant, working in small sections until you've laid all the full tiles.

Step 3

Press each tile down into the mortar with a slight twisting motion.

Step 4

A. Measure and mark the tiles that must be cut to fit, as described in step 5 of **Vinyl Tile Flooring,** pages 34-35.

B. Using a handheld tile cutter, score and snap the tiles that require only a straight cut.

C. For tiles that require notches, use a wet saw with a diamond blade or a jigsaw with a tungsten-carbide blade.

D. To cut curved lines, mark the cutting line on the tile, then use the scoring wheel of a handheld tile cutter to score several parallel lines, no more than ¼ in. apart, in the waste portion of the tile. Use tile nippers to gradually remove the scored part of the tile.

E. To cut a circular hole in a tile, score and cut the tile through the center of the hole, dividing the tile into two pieces. Use the curved method to cut each half of the hole.

Step 5

A. Apply mortar and fill in tiles in remaining quadrants. Complete each quadrant before beginning the next one.

B. Before the mortar dries completely, carefully remove the plastic spacers with needlenose pliers.

C. Cut marble threshold to fit the doorway, using a wet saw with a diamond blade or a circular saw with a masonry abrasive blade. Set the threshold so the top is even with the tile, keeping the same space between the threshold as between the tiles.

D. Let the mortar cure for 24 hours.

Step 6

A. Prepare a small batch of grout to fill the tile joints. Starting in a corner, pour the grout over the tile.

B. Use a rubber float to spread the grout outward from the corner, forcing it into the tile joints. Hold the float at a 60-degree angle and use a figure-eight motion.

C. Use the grout float to remove any excess grout from the tile surface. Continue applying grout and wiping off excess until about 25 sq. ft. of the floor has been grouted.

Step 7

A. To remove excess grout, wipe a damp grout sponge over about 2 sq. ft. of tile at a time. Wipe each area only once, to avoid pulling the grout out of the joints. Rinse the sponge in cool water between wipes.

B. Continue applying grout in this manner until the floor is completed.

Step 8

A. Allow the grout to dry for about four hours, then use a soft cloth to buff the tile surface.

B. Allow the grout to cure according to the manufacturer's instructions.

C. Apply grout sealer to all grout joints, using a small sponge or brush. Wipe any sealer from the tile surface immediately.

Step 6

Hold the float at a 60-degree angle to force grout into the joints.

VINYL TILE FLOORING

Resilient vinyl tile is often designed to mimic ceramic tile, but it's much easier to install and far less expensive. It comes in both self-adhesive and dry-back styles.

Self-adhesive tile has a wax-paper backing that you peel off as you install the tiles. Dry-back tile is secured with adhesive that you spread onto the underlayment before installing the tiles.

In this project, the instructions for positioning and cutting the tiles are the same, regardless of which type you're using. However, step 3 only applies to dry-back tiles.

Step 1
A. To establish the layout lines (X and Y), divide the room (or the largest rectangular area in the room) into equal quadrants by snapping chalklines between the center points of opposite walls.

B. Check for squareness using the 3-4-5 triangle method. From the intersection of the chalklines, measure 3 ft. along one line and make a mark. Then measure 4 ft. along the perpendicular line and make another mark. The diagonal distance between the two marks should equal 5 ft. If it doesn't, adjust the reference lines until they're exactly perpendicular to each other.

Tools
- **tape measure**
- **chalkline**
- **pencil**
- **linoleum or utility knife with extra blades**
- **straightedge**
- **tile cutter (for thick tiles)**
- **¹⁄₁₆-in. notched trowel (for dry-back tile only)**
- **hammer**

Materials
- **resilient tile**
- **flooring adhesive (for dry-back tile only)**
- **metal threshold strip**
- **nails**

Step 1

Check for squareness using the 3–4–5 triangle method.

Step 2

A. Dry-fit a row of full-size tiles along layout line Y, working from the center outward toward the walls.

B. Shift the tiles along the line as needed to make the layout look symmetrical or to reduce the number of edges that must be cut.

C. Using a different chalk color, draw a new line parallel to the original X line that runs through one of the tile joints in the Y line.

D. Keeping the first row of tiles in place, dry-fit a row of full-size tiles along the adjusted X line. Repeat step B for this line of tiles.

E. Using a different chalk color, draw a new line parallel to the original Y line that runs through one of the tile joints in the adjusted X line.

Step 3: For Dry-Back Tiles Only

A. For dry-back tile only, apply flooring adhesive around the intersection of the adjusted layout lines. Use a trowel with $1/16$-in. notches and hold it at a 45-degree angle.

B. Spread the flooring adhesive evenly over three of the quadrants in the installation area. Allow the adhesive to set according to the manufacturer's instructions.

C. To install the tile, proceed as described below, starting with step 4B. You can kneel on the tiles you've already installed to lay the new tiles.

D. When the first quadrant is completely tiled, spread the adhesive over the next quadrant, and finish setting the rest of the floor.

Step 4

A. For self-adhesive resilient tiles, peel off the paper backing as you proceed. Each time you lay a tile, rub the entire surface of the tile to bond it to the floor.

B. Install the first tile in one of the quadrants at the intersection of adjusted lines X and Y.

C. Set the tiles along the layout lines in the quadrant, keeping the joints between them tight.

D. Set all the full-size tiles tightly in the rest of that quadrant.

E. Set the full-size tiles in the other quadrants, as above—in the corner first, then on the layout lines, then in the rest of the quadrant.

Step 5

A. Mark the partial tiles in the first quadrant by laying the tile to be cut face-up on top of the last full tile you installed. Place a $1/8$-in. spacer against the wall. Set a marker tile against it, over the first tile.

B. Trace along the edge of the marker tile to draw a cutting line.

C. Cut the tile with a straightedge and a utility knife. To score and cut thick vinyl tiles, use a tile cutter.

D. Install the uncovered portion of the marked tile against the wall.

Step 6

A. Fit tiles around outside corners by making a cardboard template to match the space, allowing a $1/8$-in. gap along the walls. Cut the template and check to make sure it fits.

B. Trace the outline of the template on a tile and cut to fit. Install the cut tile against the walls.

Step 7

A. Continue installing edge tiles in the remaining quadrants, until the floor is completely covered.

B. Check the new floor; press down any loose tiles to bond them to the underfloor.

C. Install a metal threshold strip at the edges where the new floor joins another floor covering.

Install tiles along the layout lines of a quadrant first, then fill in the interior of that quadrant.

Mark the edge tiles to fit against walls. Here, the tile that will be cut is shown inverted for clarity; mark it facing up.

SHEET VINYL FLOORING

Resilient sheet vinyl offers a smooth, easy-to-clean floor at a low cost. It's available in either full-spread or perimeter-bond styles. Full-spread vinyl is secured with adhesive over the entire floor; perimeter-bond vinyl is secured only along the edges and seams. In both cases, the key to a successful floor is creating a smooth, level plywood underlayment and a perfectly cut flooring template.

Full-spread vinyl flooring bonds tightly to the floor and is unlikely to come loose. However, it's more difficult to install and requires a flawlessly smooth and clean underlayment. Perimeter-bond flooring is easier to install and will tolerate minor flaws in the underlayment, but it's also more likely to come loose.

Follow the instructions in steps 1 to 3 and step 5 for either type of sheet vinyl. In step 4, follow only the instructions for the kind of flooring you've chosen.

Step 1

A. To create a template, place sheets of heavy paper along the walls, leaving a consistent ⅛-in. gap against the wall. To secure the sheets, cut small triangular holes in them and tape them to the floor over the holes.

B. Follow the outline of the room, adding one sheet of paper at a time. Tape the edges of adjoining sheets, overlapping them by 2 in.

C. To fit the template around pipes, tape sheets of paper up to either side of the pipe. Measure the distance from the wall to the center and subtract ⅛ in.

D. Transfer the measurement to a separate piece of paper. Use a compass to draw the pipe diameter at the appropriate distance from the wall, then cut it out. Cut a slit from the edge of the paper to this hole.

Tools	Materials
• linoleum or utility knife with extra blades	• heavy butcher's or postal-wrap paper
• pencil compass	• masking tape
• scissors	• duct tape
• nonpermanent felt-tipped pen	• vinyl flooring
• ¼-in. notched trowel	• flooring adhesive
• J-roller or wallpaper seam roller (for perimeter-bond)	• ⅜-in. staples
• 100-lb. floor roller (for full-spread)	• metal threshold strip
• staple gun	• nails
• hammer	
• straightedge	

E. Fit the hole cutout around the pipe. Tape the hole template to the adjoining sheets.

F. When the template is done, roll or loosely fold it up.

Step 2

A. Sweep and vacuum the underlayment thoroughly.

B. Make sure the sheet vinyl is at room temperature. Carefully unroll it on a clean surface, taking care not to crease or fold it. Turn the sheet pattern-side up.

C. For two-piece installations, overlap the edges of the sheets by at least 2 in., matching the pattern lines. Duct-tape the sheets together.

D. Position the paper template over the flooring and tape it into place. Trace the outline of the template.

E. Remove the template. Cut the marked outlines, using a linoleum or utility knife, and a straightedge.

F. Cut the holes needed for pipes and other obstructions. Cut a slit from each hole to the edge of the flooring, cutting along a pattern line if possible.

Step 3

A. Roll up the flooring loosely and transfer it to the installation area. Unroll and position it carefully.

B. For two-piece installations, cut the seams. Hold a straightedge tightly against the flooring and cut along a pattern line through both pieces of flooring.

C. Remove both scraps. The pattern should now run continuously across the adjoining sheets.

Step 4: For Perimeter-Bond Vinyl Only

A. Fold back the seam edges of both sheets and apply a 3-in. band of adhesive to the underlayment, using a ¼-in. notched trowel.

B. Press the seam edges into the adhesive, one at a time. Make sure the seam is tight; press any gaps together with your fingers. Roll the seam edges with a J-roller. Clean any excess adhesive off immediately.

C. Apply adhesive under the cuts at the pipes and the perimeter of the room. Set the vinyl with the floor roller.

D. Fasten the outer edges of the vinyl with ⅜-in. staples driven every 3 in. Make sure the staples will be covered by the base molding.

Step 4: For Full-Spread Vinyl Only

A. Lay the flooring in place, then pull back half of the sheet and apply a layer of adhesive to the underlayment. Lay the flooring back on the adhesive.

B. Roll the flooring with the floor roller, moving from the center to the edges. Fold over the unbonded section of flooring, apply the adhesive, then lay and roll the flooring.

Step 4

For perimeter-bond flooring, apply adhesive only around the perimeter of the room and under the cuts at pipes and seams.

C. Wipe up any adhesive that oozes up around the edges, using a damp rag.

Step 5

Measure and cut metal threshold strips to fit across the doorways and any other areas where the new floor joins another floor covering. Position each strip over the edge of the flooring and nail in place.

Step 4

For full-spread flooring, lift half the sheet and apply adhesive under it. Replace the sheet and repeat on the other half.

LAMINATE FLOORING

Laminate flooring consists of a fiberboard core and a melamine surface encasing a printed photographic image that can depict almost anything. This unique material has the ability to mimic hardwoods, slate, marble, ceramic tile and other premium materials. Its versatility allows you to create custom design combinations that would ordinarily be prohibitively expensive—at a cost similar to that of simple oak strip flooring.

Laminate flooring also offers easy installation and versatility of use. For example, it can be installed over a heated floor or a basement slab. Once in place, it's durable, scratch-resistant and easy to maintain.

What to Buy

Most laminates are comparable in durability and strength, since the manufacturing process is similar. However, make sure that the floor you buy has:

- At least four layers (see **Laminate Layers** at right)
- A minimum thickness of $5/16$ in., to ensure strength and stability
- Edges sealed with water-resistant glue
- Clear installation and maintenance instructions
- A toll-free line to call with any questions
- A warranty of at least 15 years

Where to Put It

Laminate floors are floating floors; the planks or tiles aren't glued to the subfloor but to each other. This means they can go down with ease over existing floors, a plywood subfloor and even a concrete slab. Unlike solid wood, they can even be used over radiant-heat systems. However, since they have a wood-based core that will swell when wet, most aren't recommended for bathrooms, laundry rooms or other high-humidity areas.

You can choose tougher laminates for high-wear areas, such as a playroom, hallways and other heavily traveled areas, and save some money by using a less expensive flooring in the bedroom.

Installing a Laminate Floor

Installing laminate flooring in a small or average-size room is a manageable weekend project, especially if you have two people available for the gluing and assembly phase. However, unless you're quite experienced, a large room or one with a complex layout that requires significant cutting and trimming should be handled by a professional.

When installing a laminate floor, follow the manufacturer's instructions. Here are the major steps involved in laying a typical floating plank laminate floor.

Tools
- utility knife
- pencil
- chalkline
- tape measure
- flat bar
- handsaw, jigsaw or circular saw
- mallet
- plastic putty knife and spacers
- wet sponge, rag or towel

Materials
- laminate flooring planks
- wood glue
- foam backing
- masking tape

This striking floor pairs granite-look tiles with "oak" planks.

Laminate Layers

Good-quality laminate planks have at least four layers: a clear protective layer, a design image, a high-density fiberboard core and backing for added strength. Most are 7½ to 8 in. wide and 48 to 58 in. long.

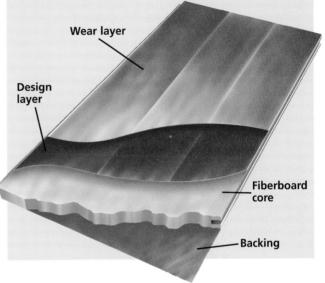

Wear layer

Design layer

Fiberboard core

Backing

Step 1

Move the flooring, still in its original cartons, into the room where it will be installed at least 48 hours before you start working to allow the planks to adjust to the room's humidity level.

Step 2

A. If necessary, trim the bottom of the door casings with a handsaw. This will allow you to slip the flooring neatly beneath the casing.

B. Roll out the foam backing and cut it to fit the room. Don't overlap the seams.

C. Lay the backing in place, securing the seams with masking tape.

Step 2

Roll out the foam backing and cut it to fit the room.

Step 3

A. Begin the installation along the longest wall. If there's a doorway or other opening across that wall, temporarily place a strip of wood or a plank across it to support the first row across the opening.

B. Place ¼-in. spacers along the wall to provide a gap in which the flooring can expand. (This gap will be covered by moldings.)

C. Dry-fit the first three rows of flooring, making sure the first row is straight. Stagger the seams in each row.

D. Cut the end pieces to fit, starting with the first three rows.

Step 4

Glue together the planks in the first three rows first, following the method described below. Allow them to cure for a few hours to provide a solid basis for the rest of the floor. Then complete the installation.

A. Apply a thin bead of wood glue to the matching grooves, tongues and end joints, according to the manufacturer's instructions. Apply the glue just before installation; it begins to set as soon as it's applied.

B. Quickly insert each tongue into the groove of the preceding row. Immediately tap the rows together tightly, using a mallet and a scrap of flooring to avoid flattening the tongue of the plank. Hold the plank tightly in place for a minute or two, until the glue sets.

C. As the glue oozes from the joints, remove it with a plastic putty knife, taking care not to scratch the flooring. Make a final pass with a clean, damp sponge, rag or towel.

Step 4

Secure the laminate planks with a thin bead of wood glue applied to the matching tongues and grooves just before you fit them together.

WHY CHOOSE LAMINATE FLOORING?

Affordable. The cost of laminate flooring is comparable to good-quality wood or vinyl flooring.

Many design options. The many designs and contrasting tiles available in laminate form make it easy to create a custom look.

Easy to install. Unless a room is large or complex, installing a laminate floor is a manageable do-it-yourself project.

Goes over existing flooring. Laminate flooring can go directly over most surfaces, including a concrete slab or a floor with a radiant-heat system.

Step 4

Tap the planks together, using a mallet and a scrap of flooring.

(Glue that's left on the floor will cause a haze on the surface.)

D. If a new plank rests higher than the previous one, weigh it down with an unopened carton of planks while the glue sets.

E. Make a cardboard template of any irregular areas, making allowances for the ¼-in. expansion gap. Trace the template onto a laminate plank and cut it to fit, using a jigsaw.

Step 5

Once the flooring is installed, extend its life by placing floor protectors under furniture, and mats at the front and back door. Use only a floor cleaner formulated for laminate floors and endorsed by the manufacturer.

Make a cardboard template to fit around irregular areas.

Manufacturers continue to develop new eye-fooling laminate designs. These ceramic-look tiles include realistic grout lines that hide the seams.

PROFESSIONAL TIPS

Here are some professional tips to consider for your laminate flooring project:

- Use your existing moldings to hide the expansion gap between the walls and the floor. Laminate companies do offer matching moldings, but they're expensive and they usually don't look as good as the existing moldings.
- The foam underlayment isn't a vapor barrier; it simply helps to reduce sound transmission. If you're installing the flooring over a concrete floor below grade, place a polyethylene vapor barrier down before you lay the foam.
- If you're installing flooring in the kitchen, use an elastomeric caulk around the edges. This flexible caulk will allow the flooring to expand and contract, while keeping spills away from the fiberboard core.

LAYERED CEILING

Tools
- hammer
- screwdriver
- straight 8-ft. 1x4 or ¼-in.-thick strip of hardboard or plywood
- drywall knife with extra blades
- paintbrush

Materials
- ½-in. drywall panels
- J-bead
- panel adhesive
- 1⅝-in. drywall screws
- joint compound
- sandpaper
- paint

Drywall can do far more than just cover wall studs and support paint, trim and wallpaper. One of the easiest and most interesting special drywall effects that you can achieve yourself is a layered ceiling. This allows you to visually define different living areas without blocking the light or the view.

In the wide-open interior shown at left, the drywall strips run in three directions from a central column, like beams. This provides a series of subtle yet effective boundaries between the living room, dining room and kitchen spaces. The added layer of drywall is edged with J-bead.

This is a simple improvement that you can install directly over an existing drywall ceiling. The J-bead is a sheet-metal molding shaped like a squared-off *J*, which you glue and screw to the edge of the drywall to provide a clean, finished edge. Here's how to do it:

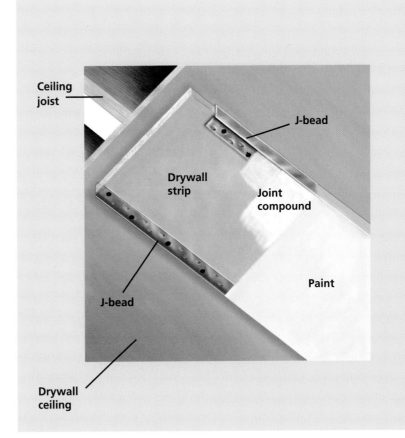

Step 1

Cut the drywall panels into 12-in.-wide strips.

A. Use a straight 8-ft.-long 1×4 (or a strip of ¼-in.-thick hardboard or plywood) as a straightedge to cut the drywall. Clamp the straightedge into position.

B. Score the line with a knife and snap the drywall. Use a utility knife to slice the paper from the back.

Step 2

A. Run a continuous bead of panel adhesive on the inside of the J-bead.

B. Press the J-bead into place on each side of one of the drywall strips.

Step 3

A. Apply two long, continuous beads of panel adhesive to the back of the first drywall strip.

B. Stick the strip in place on the ceiling.

C. Drive screws through the J-bead and the two layers of drywall, spacing the screws about 1 ft. apart. (Since the screws are only there to help secure the drywall strip, you don't need to drive them into ceiling joists.)

D. Follow steps 2A through 3C to install the rest of the drywall strips.

Step 4

A. Cover the drywall and J-bead with two or three applications of joint compound, to hide the screw heads and the lip of the J-bead, until you get a smooth finish.

B. After the joint compound is completely dry, lightly sand the surface and paint over it.

If you want the new layer to exactly match the color of the old ceiling, you'll probably need to repaint the entire ceiling.

TEXTURED CEILING

The most difficult ceiling texture to achieve is a smooth drywall finish, which requires meticulous finishing work. A textured finish is far more forgiving, and relatively easy to create on an existing drywall surface.

The variety of possible textures is limitless. Here are some of the more popular ones.

Veneer plaster allows you to give drywall ceilings and walls the solid, smooth look of old-fashioned plaster-and-lath surfaces. It goes over the drywall in one or two coats. Although it takes some practice to create a smooth trowel finish over a wide area, some people find this easier to do than conventional smooth drywall finishing.

Veneer plaster can be used to create a wide range of interesting textures. One of the most common is a skip-trowel finish, which leaves the surface roughly finished. To get a heavier finish, wait until the plaster is firm and then trowel on more plaster from the same batch. Here are some more texture ideas:

• For a rough, even texture, mix plaster with sand, and use a float to apply it over the first layer of plaster.

• For a fan or swirl pattern, arc a wallpaper brush or paintbrush across the plaster before it dries.

• To create lighter textures, use a sprayer. You can adjust it to create different effects, ranging from a splattered finish to a subtle orange-peel texture.

• To get a knockdown pattern, use a steel trowel to lightly "knock down" the peaks of a rough finish.

When it comes to creating textures, anything goes. Instead of sweeping with a brush, try a comb. Instead of floating with a trowel, try a heavy-nap roller or dab the wet plaster with anything you have on hand—a sponge, a rag or a crumpled-up plastic bag.

The easiest approach of all is to use a premixed texture finish. Roll it onto the ceiling and use a trowel or a brush to create textured effects.

SAND FLOAT

FAN PATTERN

EMBOSSED TIN CEILING

It's surprisingly easy to create a custom-designed tin ceiling that will add a striking touch to any room. You can order one from a catalog by selecting a pattern and sending in your ceiling dimensions. The company will send you back a layout that plots where each panel and plate will go.

Tin ceilings usually combine many elements (such as cornices, medallions and borders), which are actually 2 × 2-ft. or 2 × 4-ft. steel panels embossed in intricate designs. Since the nailheads are exposed, you need to use reproduction cone-head nails and half-round nailers to support the raised border designs.

Putting in a tin ceiling is a two-person job, since you're working overhead and the larger panels tend to flex. Here are the steps involved in the most common installation method.

Step 1

Nail or screw a layer of ⅜-in. plywood over the ceiling, securing it to the ceiling joists. This will provide a solid nailing surface for the ceiling panels, no matter where the seams fall.

Tools	Materials
• chalkline	• embossed ceiling panels
• hammer	• half-round nailers
• screwdriver	• cone-head nails
• large nailset	• ⅜-in. plywood
	• screws
	• paint or polyurethane varnish

Step 2

A. Measure the ceiling carefully and plan the layout of the panels.

B. Check the ceiling for squareness and adjust the layout accordingly.

C. Snap a grid of chalklines that mark the seams of the panels on the plywood. Measure carefully; the panels overlap less than ⅛ in., so there's little room for error.

Step 3

A. Secure the metal panels in place by nailing them to the plywood through the prepunched holes in the panels.

B. Working from the center of the room, tack up the first panel loosely.

C. Remove the nails from one side, overlap the next panel and firmly nail both panels in place.

D. Where the different patterns overlap, you may need to flatten some parts of the edges to bring the seams together. To do this, use a hammer and the head of a large nailset laid flat along the seam.

E. Follow the same procedure for all the remaining

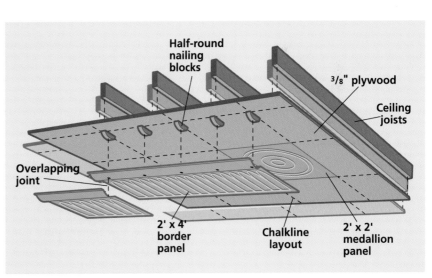

Half-round nailing blocks

Overlapping joint

3/8" plywood

Ceiling joists

2' x 4' border panel

Chalkline layout

2' x 2' medallion panel

ceiling panels.

Step 4

A. Paint the ceiling. For a one-color look, use a deep-nap roller. For a polychrome ceiling, roll on the primary color, then brush on the accents.

BEADBOARD CEILING

One of the most popular do-it-yourself ceiling finishes is tongue-and-groove beadboard paneling. A beadboard finish creates a distinctive, traditional look and draws the eye upward, which can be very effective in a small room, such as the bathroom shown here.

Before starting this project, find out which way the ceiling joists run; the boards must be installed perpendicular to them. If the ceiling is accessible from above, check the joists from the attic. From below, use an electronic stud finder, or lightly tap the ceiling with a hammer until you hear the dull thud that indicates a joist. Once you know which way the joists run, you can proceed with installing the beadboard.

Tools	Materials
• paintbrush	• beadboard
• measuring tape	• primer or stain
• chalkline	• 4d (1½-in.) finishing
• hammer	nails
• drill	• putty
• jigsaw or	• decorative molding
portable circular saw	• paint
• nailset	

Step 1

Prime or stain all the surfaces (front, back and edges) of the boards. This is critical, as it prevents moisture from passing through them and blistering the finish.

Step 2

A. Find the center of one of the ceiling joists by tapping nails into the ceiling.

B. Once you find the center, mark it and measure 16 in. over to find the next joist. (Don't worry about the marks or holes you're making in the ceiling; they'll be covered by the new paneling.)

C. Once you've located and marked all the joists, snap chalklines along the marks that indicate the center of each joist.

Step 3

A. Remove all light fixtures and turn off the electrical circuit to the work area.

B. Hold the first board up to the ceiling, perpendicular to the chalklines, with the grooved edge against the wall. If the room is wider than 8 ft., span the distance with two or more boards, placing the joints on the centerline of a joist.

C. While you're holding the first row of boards in place, have someone else measure from one end of the boards across the room to the opposite wall, and then from the other end to the opposite wall.

D. If the two measurements aren't exactly the same, adjust the position of the boards until they are. Don't worry if there's a slight gap between the first board and the wall; it will allow room for expansion and will be hidden by the molding.

Step 4

A. Holding the first board in position, drive finishing nails through the tongue and into the joist centerlines.

B. Secure the edge along the wall by face-nailing—nailing straight in through the face of the board. Only the first and last boards are face-nailed.

C. Before nailing the ends, drill pilot holes to keep the thin wood from splitting.

D. Set the nailheads.

Step 5

A. Install the second board by pressing its grooved edge over the exposed tongue of the first board. Make sure it fits tightly; hold a scrap of beadboard against the edge and tap it lightly with a hammer, taking care not to damage the tongue.

B. Secure the board by toenailing—driving nails at an angle through the tongue and into the joists. Drill pilot holes before nailing the board ends.

C. Set the nailheads below the surface, being careful not to split the tongue.

D. Install the rest of the boards, except the last one, the same way. Be sure all the joints between the boards are tight.

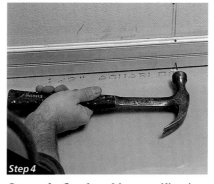

Secure the first board by toenailing into the tongue, then nailing through the face of the board along the wall.

Bore small pilot holes near the ends of the boards so the finishing nails don't split the thin wood.

Step 6

To work around light fixtures, electrical wires or other obstructions, make a paper template of the area. Transfer the markings to the boards and use a jigsaw to cut the them to fit around the obstruction.

For recessed light fixtures, use the circular cover to trace the cutting lines. Cut the boards to fit and nail them in place.

Step 7

A. Using a circular saw or jigsaw, rip the last board lengthwise to fit along the wall. Don't fit it tightly to the wall; the beadboard needs room to expand.

B. Slip the last board into place and face-nail it to the joists.

C. Set all the nailheads just below the surface.

D. Fill the nailheads with putty.

Step 8

A. Install a decorative molding to hide the gaps around the edges of the ceiling.

Flat moldings, such as doorstop, base cap and cove, are easy to install but don't look as elegant as a classic crown molding. (However, see pages 18-19 for a simple, do-it-yourself crown molding project.)

B. Apply a final coat of paint to the beadboard and the molding.

Finish by installing crown (shown) or other molding. Apply a final coat of paint.

Making Baths Work Better

*Transform your
tub and shower into
an attractive,
welcoming place to
linger and relax.*

Making Baths Work Better

QUICK REFERENCE

SHOWERS	*Porcelain Soap Dish*	*page 52*
	Slide-Bar Showerhead	*page 53*
	Shower Seat	*page 54*
BATHTUBS	*Glass Tub Enclosure*	*page 56*
	Solid-Surface Tub Surround	*page 58*

Improving a bathroom doesn't need to be expensive or complicated. You can easily upgrade your existing tub or shower by adding a few extra details that will enhance its safety, practicality and attractiveness.

The suggestions in this chapter require only a modest investment of time and money, but they do call for a range of skill levels. While installing a porcelain soap dish is a good project for a beginner, installing a tiled shower seat requires more advanced skills.

While none of these projects is particularly difficult, it's advisable to develop a modest level of carpentry skill before you tackle them. If you haven't worked with caulk before, it's also a good idea to practice first, until you have complete confidence in your ability to create watertight seals.

The most important factor for success with the projects in this chapter is making sure you have the correct materials. If you start with the right tools and supplies, the work should go smoothly.

Regardless of your skills and experience, it's a good idea to have a partner assist you with installing the larger projects—the pieces involved are bulky and may be difficult to handle alone.

Showers

When positioned properly—out of range of the shower spray—a porcelain soap dish can be a handy addition to a shower. In the first project you'll see that installing a soap dish can be as simple as replacing a tile.

The slide-bar showerhead featured next combines the convenience and flexibility of a fixed and a handheld showerhead, and can be adjusted to any height. If you have some basic plumbing knowledge, installing this fixture should be quite easy.

A shower seat provides a sturdy place to sit while bathing, which is especially helpful for an elderly bather. Here, we show you how to simplify the installation of a shower seat with a kit that's available at specialty tile shops. It includes a triangular pan that's attached directly to the wall, filled with mortar and then covered to match the existing wall tiles.

Probably the most difficult of this trio of projects, the shower seat requires moderate construction skills and some experience with installing ceramic tile.

Bathtubs

The glass tub and shower enclosure featured here offers total access to the tub, because it has no horizontal rails. Its unique panels slide and pivot independently, providing a variety of ways to access the tub.

Solid surfacing, a popular choice for kitchen countertops, is also useful in the bathroom. In the last project in this chapter, we show you how to install vertical-grade solid surfacing over your existing tub and shower walls and use matching moldings to create a finished look.

PORCELAIN SOAP DISH

A porcelain soap dish installed on the shower wall is a good way to keep your soap from getting soggy—as long as the dish is in the right position. Place the dish high on the wall to keep the soap safe from shower spray.

Pick a dish that matches the color and finish of your existing wall tile. If your shower walls are covered with a fiberglass or acrylic surround, buy a soap dish that can be glued right to the wall. Be sure to use the recommended adhesive, or you may permanently damage the shower surround.

Tools
- eye protection
- grout saw or awl
- hammer
- nailset
- drill
- ¼-in.-dia. masonry drill bit
- cold chisel
- putty knife or notched trowel

Materials
- 4x4-in. or 4x6-in. porcelain soap dish
- tile adhesive
- tile grout
- masking tape

Step 2

Bore a series of holes through the tile but not into the wall surface behind it.

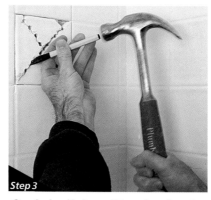

Step 3

Crack the tile by striking the edge of each hole with a chisel and hammer.

Step 4

Spread the tile adhesive onto the wall and scratch in a series of ridges.

Step 1
A. First, choose the best place on the wall to put the soap dish.

Choose a spot that's four or five tiles below the showerhead (about 16 to 20 in.) and two or three tiles to the right or left of it (about 8 to 10 in.).

B. Identify the tile that you will replace with the soap dish.

A 4×4-in. soap dish requires one tile space; a 4×6-in. dish requires 1½ tile spaces.

Step 2
A. Wearing eye protection, scratch out the grout from around the tile, using a grout saw or awl.

B. Use a hammer and nailset to punch a series of divots across the face of the tile in an *X* pattern.

C. Using the divots as starting points, bore through the tile, but not the wall behind it, with a ¼-in.-dia. masonry drill bit.

Step 3
A. Crack the tile into smaller pieces by striking the edge of each hole with a ¼-in.-wide cold chisel and a hammer.

B. Pry out the fractured shards of tile. Scrape the wall surface clean of any old mortar or leftover adhesive.

Step 4
A. Spread a thin coat of tile adhesive onto the wall and the back of the soap dish, using a putty knife or notched trowel. If you're using a putty knife, scratch ridges into the adhesive.

B. Firmly press the dish into place and secure it with two or three strips of masking tape. Check to make sure the dish is level.

Step 5
A. Wait 24 hours, then fill all the joints around the soap dish with grout.

B. Allow the grout to dry overnight before using the shower.

SLIDE-BAR SHOWERHEAD

A sliding showerhead is an attractive and practical shower addition, since it combines the convenience of a fixed showerhead with the flexibility of a handheld sprayer.

The model shown here has a 2-ft.-long vertical bar with an adjustable slide-lock mechanism. The showerhead can be positioned anywhere on the bar, or lifted off and used as a handheld sprayer.

Step 1

A. Select a slide-bar showerhead that matches your bath fixtures.

B. Remove the existing showerhead with a pipe wrench. If you plan to reuse it, protect its finish by wrapping it in a cloth.

Step 2

A. Wrap the threads of the brass nipple with Teflon tape.

B. Thread it into the stub-out in the wall. Leave about 9/16 in. of the nipple protruding from the wall.

C. Carefully thread the chrome wall supply elbow onto the nipple.

D. Cover the elbow with a soft cloth and tighten it with a pipe wrench (or use a strap wrench).

Step 3

A. Press a mounting bracket onto each end of the slide bar.

Tools
- pipe wrench or strap wrench
- soft cloth
- 3/16-in.-dia. masonry drill bit
- 1/2-in.-dia. masonry drill bit
- screwdriver
- level
- nailset
- hammer
- drill

Materials
- slide-bar showerhead kit
- 1/2-in.-dia. x 1 1/2-in.-long brass nipple
- Teflon tape
- hollow-wall anchor or toggle bolt
- 1/4-20 machine screws

B. Place the bar 4 to 6 in. to the side of the wall supply elbow; the lowest end of the bar should be about 52 in. above the bottom of the tub or shower.

C. Hold the bar against the wall and check it for plumb with a level.

Step 4

A. Outline the screw holes in the brackets on the wall.

B. Use a hammer and nailset to start the screw holes. Drill the holes with a 3/16-in.-dia. masonry drill bit.

C. If you hit a stud, attach the slide bar directly to the wall.

D. If you don't hit a stud, use a 1/2-in. masonry drill bit to enlarge the hole. Insert a hollow-wall anchor or toggle bolt into the hole.

E. Slide the retainer ring forward to hold the fastener against the back of the wall. Snap off the plastic straps.

Step 5

A. Attach the slide bar to the wall with screws driven through the mounting brackets and into the wall. If you're fastening the bar to a stud, use the screws provided with the kit. If you're using toggle bolts, attach it with 1/4-20 machine screws.

B. Conceal the screws by sliding chrome-finished end caps onto the upper and lower mounting brackets.

C. Thread the flexible steel hose onto the wall supply elbow. Clip the showerhead into the slide-lock mechanism.

Step 2

Thread the chrome-plated wall supply elbow onto the nipple and tighten.

Step 4

Insert the toggle bolt into the hole and slide the retainer ring forward.

SHOWER SEAT

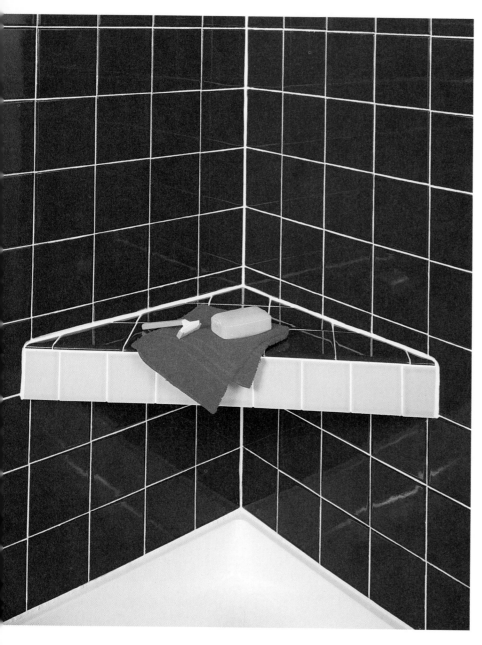

This attractive shower seat is built with a kit that greatly simplifies the installation. It provides an attractive, secure place to sit during a shower, and can also serve as a handy shelf.

Because of the kit, you don't have to tear open the wall, break up any tile or build a wooden frame. The kit includes a triangular aluminum pan that's fastened directly to the existing wall, then filled with mortar and covered with ceramic tile. Ask for it at specialty tile shops.

Tools
- tape measure
- masking tape
- felt-tip marker
- drill
- ⅜-in.-dia. carbide-tip masonry drill bit
- screwdriver
- mortar trowel
- tile cutter
- trowel with ⅛-in. notches
- rubber float

Materials
- shower seat kit
- masonry mortar mix
- tiles
- thin-set mortar or latex mastic
- grout
- sponge
- soft cloth
- silicone caulk

Step 1

Determine where you want to install the shower seat and how high you want to put it on the wall. For most adults, the most comfortable position will be about 16 to 20 in. above the shower floor.

Step 2

A. Hold the metal pan in position on the wall. Place a strip of masking tape on the wall at the locations of the six screw holes. (The tape will make marking the holes easier and will help keep the drill bit from spinning off the marks.)

B. Using a felt-tip marker, outline the screw holes on the tape.

C. Drill through the wall at each mark, using a ⅜-in.-dia. carbide-tip masonry bit. Remove the tape.

D. Insert the hollow-wall screw anchors provided with the kit partway into the holes.

(The anchors open as the screws are tightened, attaching the seat securely to the wall. If you hit a stud while boring the anchor holes, use a 2½-in. wood screw instead.)

E. Place a dab of silicone caulk around each anchor head, to seal out water, then press the anchors all the way in.

Tighten the screws in the wall anchors to secure the pan to the wall.

Step 3

A. Hold the metal pan in position on the wall.

B. Insert the screws through the holes and into the wall anchors. Tighten the screws until the bench is securely fastened to the wall.

C. Apply a thin bead of silicone caulk along the top edge of the bench.

Step 4

A. Mix the masonry mortar according to the manufacturer's instructions.

B. Use a trowel to pack the mortar tightly into all three corners, until it comes out of the holes in the front. Smooth the top surface.

C. Trowel a thin, wetter coat of mortar onto the front edge of the bench.

D. Let the mortar cure for at least 24 hours.

Step 5

Cover the top of the bench with tile that matches the shower walls (you can also use a slab of stone or solid-surface material). If you like, you can trim the front edge with smaller tiles.

A. Dry-lay a full tile in the center of the bench, allowing it to overhang the front edge by about ¼ in.

B. Dry-lay the remaining full tiles, working out in both directions and back to the corner.

C. Use a tile cutter to trim the tiles that abut the walls. Dry-lay the cut tiles around the full tiles.

Step 6

A. Remove all the tiles. Spread thin-set mortar or premixed latex

mastic over the top and front edges of the bench, using a trowel with ⅛-in. notches.

B. Lay the top-surface tiles first, then the edge tiles. Firmly press down on each tile to set it. Allow to cure overnight.

Step 7

A. Press grout into the joints between tiles with a rubber float, spreading the grout over the entire surface of the tile. To completely seal out moisture, you need to force the grout into every crack.

B. Let the grout set for about 20 minutes, then wipe off the excess with a damp sponge.

C. Once the grout is dry and hard, buff the tile with a soft, dry cloth.

D. Allow the grout to cure for at least 24 hours.

Step 8

A. Run a thin bead of silicone caulk around the perimeter of the bench, to seal out water.

B. Let the caulk set for six to eight hours before you use the shower.

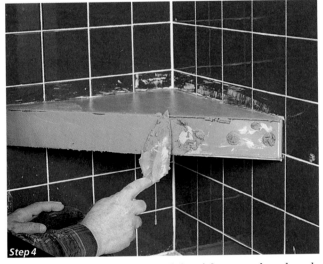

Fill the pan with mortar, smooth it with a trowel, and apply a thinner coat to the front edge of the bench.

Lay the top-surface tiles first, then the edge tiles. Press down firmly on each tile to set it into the mortar or mastic.

GLASS TUB ENCLOSURE

This attractive glass-and-aluminum tub enclosure has four narrow tempered glass panels that slide or pivot independently, allowing you to access the tub and shower in a variety of convenient ways.

For a small opening, you simply slide open the two center panels. To access the whole tub at once, slide open the center panels and pull the doubled-up panels outward into the room.

The panels will also pivot inward, which comes in handy in tiny bathrooms or when you're cleaning the tub or shower. Since the glass panels are supported by vertical jambs mounted to the side walls, there are no horizontal rails to clean around or duck under.

Step 2

At each screw location, bore a hole through the tile and wallboard, then tap in a screw anchor.

Tools
- level
- hammer
- nailset
- drill
- ¼-in.-dia. masonry drill bit
- screwdriver

Materials
- glass tub enclosure
- plastic wall anchors
- 1¼-in. screws
- ½-in. screws
- clear silicone caulk

Step 1
A. Hold one of the aluminum wall jambs against the wall to which it will be attached. Use a level to make sure it's plumb.

B. Mark the six screw holes onto the wall.

C. Repeat for the other jamb.

Step 2
A. If the wall is tiled, use a hammer and a nailset to make a small divot at each screw hole.

B. Bore a ¼-in.-dia. hole through the wall at each divot.

C. Insert plastic wall anchors into the holes. Gently tap them in with a hammer. (If you hit a stud, use 2½-in. wood screws instead of wall anchors.)

Step 3

A. Hold the jamb in place and secure it with six 1¼-in. screws driven into the anchors.

B. Repeat for the other jamb.

C. Check to make sure the jambs are plumb. If they aren't, loosen the screws, tap the jambs into alignment and retighten the screws.

Step 4

A. Lay one of the panel assemblies on its side.

B. Apply clear silicone caulk to the underside of the pivot block that sits on the tub ledge. Be careful not to get any caulk on the glass panels.

Step 5

A. Hold the panel assembly a few inches above the tub ledge and push the pivot block down over the wall jamb.

B. Carefully lower the entire panel assembly down onto the tub ledge.

C. Secure the panels by driving two ½-in. screws through the pre-bored holes in the panel frame and into the wall jamb.

D. Repeat the above steps to prepare and install the other panel assembly.

Step 6

A. Test the glass panels to see how smoothly they slide and pivot.

B. If necessary, raise or lower them by turning the top roller bracket screws.

C. Apply a bead of clear silicone caulk along the vertical joints where the frame meets the wall.

D. Apply a bead of clear silicone caulk along the inside and outside of the frame.

Hold the panel assembly above the tub ledge, press it to the wall, and lower it.

If the glass panels don't slide smoothly, adjust the screws in the top roller bracket.

SOLID-SURFACE TUB SURROUND

Durable solid surfacing has long been popular for kitchen countertops—and it works just as well as a tub surround. Here we demonstrate how it can give a shower enclosure a facelift in one weekend.

This project uses ⅛-in. solid-surface veneer to cover the tile walls around a 5-ft. tub. It comes in a kit that includes two 30×60-in. wall panels, one 60×60-in. wall panel and matching trim molding.

Although these wall panels extend all the way to the ceiling, that isn't typical; they usually stop 18 to 22 in. short of it. However, you can use the installation method shown here for any wall.

Step 1

Inspect the existing wall. Solid-surface panels can be glued to almost any surface that's flat, structurally sound and completely clean. If there are any loose tiles, pry them off and reinstall them with ceramic-tile adhesive. If more than 10 percent of the tiles are loose, remove them all and cover the wall with cement backerboard or water-resistant drywall.

Step 2

A. Lay cardboard or an old blanket on the tub bottom to protect it.

B. Remove the showerhead, tub spout and faucet handles. Use a cold chisel and a hammer to knock off any wall-mounted towel racks and soap dishes.

C. Wearing eye protection and a dust mask or respirator, remove caked-on dirt and soap scum from the tiles by scuff-sanding them with a random-orbit sander fitted with 80-grit sandpaper.

D. Use a damp rag to wipe away the sanding dust.

Tools
- cold chisel
- hammer
- random-orbit sander fitted with 80-grit sandpaper
- portable circular saw, or router & carbide-tipped straight bit with top-mounted ball-bearing pilot & straight-edge guide
- caulk gun
- J-roller
- drill
- hole saw
- scissors
- plastic trowel with ⅛-in. notches

Materials
- solid-surface tub-surround kit to fit the size of your tub
- cardboard or blanket (tub liner)
- cardboard (template)
- silicone adhesive
- ¹⁄₁₆-in. shims

Test-fit the cardboard template over the holes in the plumbing-end wall.

Step 3

A. Measure the three walls.

B. If necessary, trim the wall panels to fit. Cut them about ⅛ in. less than the width and height of the existing wall.

To trim the panels, you can use a circular saw, but a router and a carbide-tipped straight bit with a top-mounted ball-bearing pilot will give you quicker, cleaner cuts. Clamp a straightedge guide to the panel and move the router from left to right. The ball-bearing pilot will ride against the straightedge guide and produce a perfectly straight cut.

Step 4

A. Make a cardboard template of the plumbing, indicating the exact position of the showerhead pipe, tub spout and faucet handle stems. Transfer these marks to the cardboard and cut out the holes.

B. Test-fit the cardboard template to make sure the holes align exactly with the pipes in the wall.

Step 5

Install the large panel to the back wall of the tub.

A. Using a caulk gun, apply a continuous ¼-in. bead of silicone adhe-

sive to the entire wall in a grid of horizontal and vertical lines, spaced about 6 in. apart.

B. Apply a double bead of adhesive along the top and bottom of the wall for extra holding power.

C. Spread the adhesive across the wall, using a plastic trowel with ⅛-in.-wide notches.

D. Immediately press the panel into the wall. Place 1/16-in.-thick shims under the panel to hold it above the top of the tub.

E. Go over the entire surface firmly with a J-roller to set the panel into the adhesive.

Step 6

A. To cut the plumbing-end panel, place the cardboard template over the panel and mark all the holes.

B. Remove the template; drill out the holes, using a hole saw for smaller holes and a router and straight bit for larger holes.

C. Test-fit the panel to make sure that it fits over the pipes.

D. Spread adhesive on the wall, as in steps 5A to 5C.

E. Press the panel into place, making sure the holes line up properly. Go over it firmly with a J-roller.

F. Repeat steps 6D and 6E for the opposite end panel.

Step 7

A. Measure the back wall.

B. Cut a piece of molding ⅛ in. less than that length to allow the trim to expand without buckling.

C. Apply adhesive to the back of the molding and press it to the wall. Use several strips of masking tape to hold it in place.

D. Repeat steps 7A to 7C for the two end walls.

E. Cut and install the vertical corner trim in the same way. Again, hold it in place with masking tape.

Press the plumbing-end panel in place, making sure the holes align correctly with the showerhead, the tub spout and the faucet.

Step 8

A. On some tub surrounds, the tile extends an inch or so beyond the end panels. To conceal it, form a corner trim from two flat pieces of solid-surface molding joined at a 90-degree angle.

B. Glue the molding to the tile with silicone adhesive.

C. Allow the adhesive to dry for 24 hours before removing the tape or using the tub.

Conceal the outer rim of the wall tile with two molding pieces joined together at a 90-degree angle.

MAKING BATHS WORK BETTER

Lighting Up Your Home

❧

*Brighten your home
with this resourceful
collection of
lighting, window and
skylight projects.*

❧

Lighting Up Your Home

QUICK REFERENCE		
LIGHTING	Dimmer Switches	page 64
	Specialty Switches	page 65
	Recessed Lighting	page 66
	Ceiling Fan–Light	page 68
WINDOWS	Weatherizing Windows	page 70
	Replacing Sashes	page 72
	Interior Shutters	page 74
	Glass Block Window	page 76
SKYLIGHTS	Tubular Skylight	page 80

Light is perhaps the one element of a room that's essential to both its visual appeal and its function as a living space. The play of natural and artificial light in a room can be multiplied indirectly by using mirrors (see **Mirrors,** pages 22-27). However, the most direct way to enhance the light in a room is to add or improve light fixtures, windows and skylights.

Lighting

This section describes three kinds of projects: installing new switches, replacing a recessed light fixture and converting an overhead fixture to a fan-light.

There are many different kinds of dimmer and specialty switches on the market. Here we show how easy it is to install new switches that can make it more convenient to control your light fixtures.

These projects are very simple, even if you've never worked with electrical circuits before. Just follow the safety steps that are described for each project.

Replacing a recessed light fixture and installing a ceiling fan-light are somewhat more challenging projects, but they won't present any serious difficulties if you've done electrical work before.

The ceiling fan-light installation is the most difficult project in this section, and if you need to build a ceiling brace to secure the fixture, it will also require solid carpentry skills.

Windows

Windows are our link with the outside world; they let in the air and light that brighten our homes. Adding, remodeling or upgrading a window can do wonders for a room.

This section includes four projects: weatherizing windows, replacing sashes, installing interior shutters and installing a glass block window.

If you're comfortable with power tools and familiar with do-it-yourself carpentry techniques, you'll enjoy improving your home with these projects.

Skylights

Skylights are a wonderful way to brighten a dark room, but they do have some drawbacks—they tend to be energy-inefficient and difficult to install. However, there's a new kind of skylight that comes preassembled in a tube and minimizes both of these problems.

Tubular skylights are far more energy-efficient than regular skylights and can be installed in one weekend. Since the flexible tube channels light into the house through a reflective interior coating, the tube doesn't need to travel in a straight line, and you can maneuver it to get around obstructions and tight spaces in the attic. Also, since you don't need to build a shaft, you don't have to do any of the drywall or painting work required for a regular skylight.

DIMMER SWITCHES

Dimmer Switches

A dimmer switch allows you to adjust the brightness of the light fixture to any level you wish—and replacing a regular switch with a dimmer is a very easy electrical project. You can replace any standard single-pole switch with a dimmer, as long as the switch box is big enough.

Here are the general instructions for this project; however, if the manufacturer's instructions for your dimmer switch differ from these, follow them instead.

Tools
- screwdriver
- neon circuit tester
- combination tool

Materials
- twist-on wire connectors
- fine sandpaper
- dimmer switches

Step 1

A. Turn off the power to the switch at the service panel.

B. Remove the switch coverplate and the mounting screws. Pull the switch from the box, holding it by the mounting straps. Don't touch the bare wires or screw terminals.

Step 2

A. Touch one probe of a neon circuit tester to the grounded metal box or the bare copper grounding wires. Touch the other probe to each screw terminal.

If you're replacing an existing dimmer, insert the second probe into each of the wire connectors, in turn.

B. If the tester glows, it means there's still power running to the switch. Return to the service panel and shut off the correct circuit.

Step 3

A. Once you've confirmed that the power is off, disconnect the circuit wires and remove the switch.

B. Straighten the circuit wires and check them. If the ends are darkened or dirty, clean them with fine sandpaper. If they're nicked, clip them with a combination tool.

C. Use the combination tool to strip about ½ in. of clean bare wire.

Step 4

A. Connect the wire leads on the dimmer switch to either of the circuit wires, using wire connectors.

B. If you're installing a three-way dimmer, it will also have an additional wire lead, called a common wire. Attach it to the darkest screw terminal.

Step 5

A. Mount the switch in the electical box, tucking the wires in carefully.

B. Reattach the switch coverplate.

C. Restore the power to the switch at the main service panel.

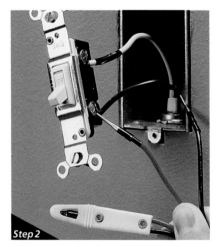

Use a neon circuit tester to test the connection to make sure the power is off.

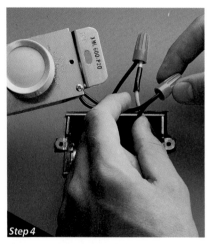

Connect the wire leads on the dimmer to the circuit wires.

SPECIALTY SWITCHES

Automatic Switches

Automatic switches are especially convenient for children, the elderly and those with physical disabilities. They have an infrared beam that detects nearby movement—such as a passing hand—and signals the switch to turn on or off. Some also include a manual dimmer.

Step 1

Follow steps 1 to 3 under **Dimmer Switches**, page 64.

Step 2

Connect the black wire leads on the specialty switch to the black (hot) circuit wires. If the box also has white neutral wires, connect them to each other with a wire connector. Connect the bare copper grounding wires to the grounding wire from the metal box, as shown.

Step 3

Follow step 5 under **Dimmer Switches**, page 64.

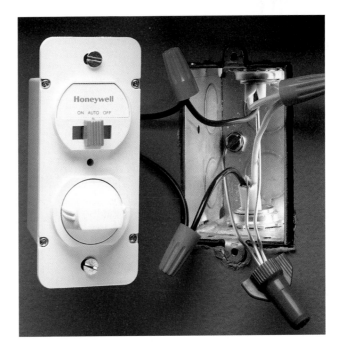

Motion-Sensing Switches

Motion-sensing switches have a wide-angle infrared beam that turns on a light fixture whenever it detects movement in the room. Most have a manual override, and some have a sensitivity control and a time-delay shutoff.

Step 1

Follow steps 1 to 3 under **Dimmer Switches**, page 64.

Step 2

Follow step 2 under **Automatic Switches,** above.

Step 3

Follow step 5 under **Dimmer Switches**, page 64.

Programmable Switches

Programmable switches are a good idea whenever you have to leave your home unoccupied. They can recall up to four on-off cycles a day. To make a home look active, they should ideally be set in a random on-off pattern.

Step 1

Follow steps 1 to 3 under **Dimmer Switches**, page 64.

Step 2

Follow step 2 under **Automatic Switches,** above.

Step 3

Follow step 5 under **Dimmer Switches**, page 64.

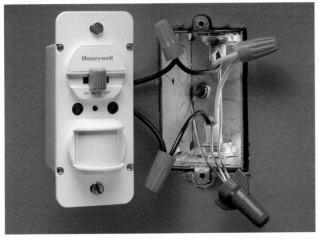

Motion-sensing switches turn light fixtures on when they detect any movement in the room.

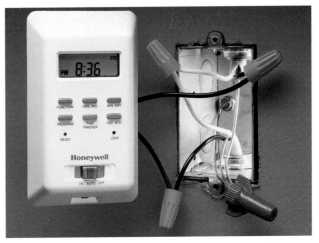

The automatic controls of a programmable switch offer an invaluable safety feature when you're away from home.

RECESSED LIGHTING

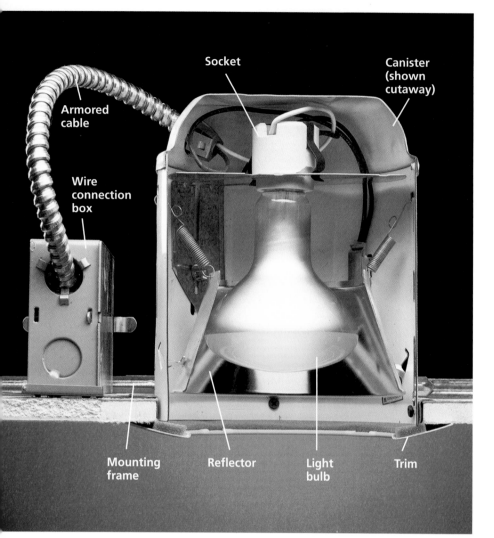

Socket

Canister (shown cutaway)

Armored cable

Wire connection box

Mounting frame

Reflector

Light bulb

Trim

Step 1

Turn off the power to the recessed light fixture at the service panel. Don't just turn off the switch—voltage may continue to leak through the wires and cause a shock. Instead, turn the light on and follow these steps:

If your electrical circuits are labeled, locate the breaker or fuse in the service panel that controls the fixture's circuit, and turn it off. The light should go out.

If your circuits aren't labeled, go to the circuit box and turn off each circuit in turn until the light goes out.

Don't touch any bare wires until you've confirmed that there is no power to the circuit (step 3).

Step 2

A. Remove the trim, the bulb and the reflector, which is held in place by springs or mounting clips.

B. Loosen the screws or clips that hold the canister to the mounting frame. Carefully raise the canister and set it aside inside the ceiling cavity.

C. Remove the coverplate on the

Light fixtures that are recessed into the ceiling can provide a range of lighting effects, from subtle to dramatic, to complement the decor of your home. However, replacing a recessed light fixture is somewhat more complicated than replacing a standard ceiling-mounted fixture.

It's easiest to replace a recessed light if you get a new fixture that's the same model as the old one, because this means that you'll be able to install the new one in the existing metal canister.

Recessed fixtures that are marked "I.C." can be placed right up against the attic insulation. All other recessed lighting canisters must be kept at least 3 in. away from any insulation—if they get any closer, they'll trap heat, which can melt the insulation on the socket wires and cause the fixture to fail or even catch fire.

As with any electrical repair, follow the manufacturer's instructions and commonsense rules of electrical safety. Here are the steps involved in safely evaluating and replacing a recessed light fixture.

Tools
• screwdriver
• neon circuit tester
• continuity tester

Materials
• recessed light fixture
• twist-on wire connectors

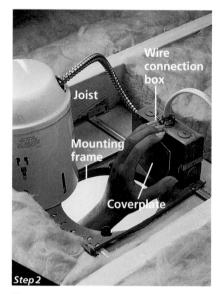

Wire connection box

Joist

Mounting frame

Coverplate

Step 2

Remove the coverplate on the wire connection box.

wire connection box, which is attached to the mounting frame between the ceiling joists. Be careful not to touch any bare wires.

Step 3

A. Test to make sure the power is off: touch one probe of the circuit tester to the grounded wire connection box and insert the other probe into each wire connector. If the tester doesn't light, it's safe to continue working and touch the bare wires.

B. If the tester glows at any point during the test, it means that power is still reaching the fixture. Return to the service panel and shut off circuits until the tester no longer lights.

Step 4

A. Once you're sure that the power is off, disconnect the black and white circuit wires by twisting off the wire connectors holding the matched pairs together.

B. Pull the armored cable from the wire connection box.

C. Remove the canister through the frame opening.

D. Lift out the socket.

E. Adjust the metal tab at the bottom of the fixture by prying it up slightly with a small screwdriver. This will improve its contact with the light bulb.

Step 5

Test the socket with a continuity tester to make sure it's operating correctly.

A. Place the clip of the continuity tester on the exposed end of the black wire while touching its metal probe to the metal tab.

B. Place the clip of the continuity tester on the exposed end of the white wire while touching its metal probe to the threaded metal socket.

C. The tester should glow during both tests. If it doesn't, it means that the socket is defective and needs to be replaced.

Step 6

A. Set the new canister inside the hole in the ceiling.

B. Thread its wires through the hole in the wire connection box.

C. Push the armored cable into

the wire connection box to secure it (it should snap into place).

Step 7

A. Connect the white fixture wire to the white circuit wire, using a twist-on wire connector.

B. Connect the black fixture wire to the black circuit wire, using a twist-on wire connector.

C. Attach the coverplate to the wire connection box.

D. Unless the fixture is marked "I.C.," take care to keep any insulation at least 3 in. away from the canister and the connection box.

Step 8

A. Position the canister inside the mounting frame.

B. Attach the mounting screws or clips. Attach the reflector and trim.

C. Install a light bulb of the proper wattage.

D. Restore power to the fixture at the main service panel.

E. Check to make sure that the new fixture is working properly.

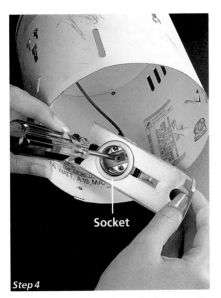

Pry up the metal tab at the bottom of the fixture with a screwdriver.

Push the armored cable into the wire connection box.

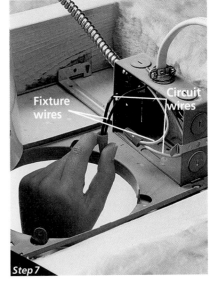

Connect the fixture wires to the circuit wires with twist-on wire connectors.

LIGHTING UP YOUR HOME

CEILING FAN-LIGHT

In addition to adding a touch of elegance, an investment in a ceiling fan-light will pay off year-round by cooling the room in the summer and circulating trapped heat downward in the winter. Some models, such as this one, also have a remote control feature. You can install the fan-light yourself if you use the wiring for an existing ceiling fixture, as shown here.

Tools
- neon circuit tester
- screwdriver
- drill
- 5/16-in.-dia. drill bit

Materials
- ceiling fan-light fixture
- 2x6 brace or expandable ceiling fan brace
- 3-in. screws
- 1/4-in.-dia. x 4-in.-long lag screws
- twist-on wire connectors
- electrical tape
- 40W light bulbs (2)
- 9V battery

Step 1
Leave the existing light on and turn off the power to the fixture at the service panel. Don't just turn off the switch—voltage may still leak through. When you turn off the correct circuit, the light will go out.

Step 2
A. If the old fixture has a glass globe, remove it and take out the light bulbs.

B. Unscrew the fixture from the electrical box; support it carefully while you disconnect it by twisting off the wire connectors. Don't touch any bare wires.

C. Touch the bare wires with the probe of a neon circuit tester.

D. If the tester doesn't light, it's safe to begin working. If the tester lights, power is still running to the fixture. Return to the service panel and shut off the correct circuit.

Step 3
A. Determine whether the electrical box is firmly attached to a support brace that's secured to the joists. Never hang a fan from an unbraced box—it can pull out of the ceiling.

B. If there's no support brace in place, install one above the electrical box by cutting a piece of 2×6 lumber to fit beween the joists.

C. If the ceiling is accessible from above, push the brace down over the electrical box. Secure it by driving 3-in. screws through the joists and into the ends of the brace.

D. If the ceiling isn't accessible from above, you have two options. You can cut out a section of the ceiling, screw a support brace in place above the electrical box and then patch and paint the ceiling. Or you can install an expandable metal brace through the hole for the electrical box.

Step 4
A. Drill two 5/16-in.-dia. holes through the electrical box only. Continue by drilling 3/16-in.-dia. pilot holes into the support brace.

B. Attach the plate with two lag screws driven through the hole in the box and into the brace.

Secure the ceiling plate to the support brace with two lag screws.

Step 5

A. Gather the six wire leads from the fan motor.

B. Feed them through the holes in the brass-plated canopy and the pipe nipple.

C. Thread the nipple into the motor housing and tighten the setscrew to lock it in place.

D. Lift the fan motor and hang it onto the hook that protrudes from the ceiling plate.

Step 6

A. Place the receiver for the remote control inside the canopy.

B. Begin connecting the wires as shown in the instructions, joining pairs of same-color wires with twist-on wire connectors. Wrap each connection with electrical tape.

C. The one remaining wire, a thin white strand, is the remote antenna. Pull it out through the slot in the ceiling plate and let it hang out.

Step 7

A. Tuck the wires into the electrical box. Wind up any excess wires and place them on top of the receiver.

B. Lift the fan motor by the canopy and slide it onto the mounting screws protruding from the side of the ceiling plate. Don't let any

Thread the wire leads through the canopy and the pipe nipple.

wires stick out from the canopy.

C. Tighten the mounting screw.

Step 8

A. Install the fan blades by sliding them one by one through the slots in the rotating ring, or belly band.

B. Secure each blade, using the hardware provided.

C. Attach the fan-light fixture by snapping together the electrical fitting.

D. Screw in two 40W light bulbs. Install the glass globe.

E. Put a 9V battery in the hand-held remote-control transmitter.

Step 9

A. Restore the electrical power at the service panel.

B. Test to make sure that the fan and the light are operating properly.

C. Secure the wall-mounted remote holder in place with screws.

Slip the receiver for the remote control into the canopy.

Let the white antenna wire hang out to receive the transmitter signal.

Insert the fan blades through the rotating ring below the motor housing.

WEATHERIZING WINDOWS

Sealing the heat loss areas around a window can increase its energy efficiency by 100 percent by creating a dead air space between the inner and outer panes. Modern double- and triple-paned windows contain inert gases between the panes to help create such air spaces. You can create a similar effect in older windows by adding weatherstripping and a good storm window (or plastic window sheeting) to block the movement of air. This keeps warm, moist air inside the window, minimizing condensation and frost buildup between the window and the storm. Here's how to do it properly.

Weatherizing Double-Hung Windows
Step 1

A. Cut V-channel (metal tension) weatherstripping to fit in the sliding sash channels. Cut it so that it extends at least 2 in. past the closed position but doesn't cover the sash-closing mechanisms.

B. Attach the V-channel by driving wire brads (which usually come with it) through it and into the sash channel with a tack hammer. Drive the fasteners flush with the surface, so the sliding sash won't catch on them.

C. Flare out the open ends of the V-channel with a putty knife, so the channel is slightly wider than the gap between the sash and the track it fits into. Don't flare too much at one time—pressing the channel back together may cause buckling.

Tools
- tack hammer
- putty knife
- hair dryer
- staple gun

Materials
- V-channel (metal tension) weatherstripping
- compressible foam weatherstripping
- tubular gasket strips
- reinforced felt strips
- wire brads
- self-adhesive foam
- caulk backer rope

Step 1

Double-hung windows: Cut a metal V-channel to fit in the channels for the sliding sash.

Step 1

Double-hung windows: Use a putty knife to flare out the open ends of the V-channel.

Step 2

A. Wipe down the underside of the bottom window sash with a damp rag and allow it to dry.

B. Attach self-adhesive compressible foam or rubber to the underside of the sash. If possible, use hollow tubular gasket strips, which create an airtight seal when the window is locked into position.

Step 3

A. To seal the gap between the top sash and the bottom sash, start by lifting the bottom sash and lowering the top sash. Tack metal V-channel to the bottom rail of the top sash, using wire brads. Be sure to point the open end of the "V" downward, so moisture won't be able to collect in the channel.

B. Flare out the V-channel with a putty knife to fit the gap between the sashes.

Weatherizing Storm Windows

After installing a storm window, fill any gaps between the exterior window trim and the storm window with caulk backer rope. Create a tight seal by attaching foam compression strips to the outside of the storm window stops.

During cold weather, check the inside surface of the storm window for condensation or frost buildup, which are caused by moisture trapped between the storm window and the permanent window. To allow the trapped moisture to escape, drill one or two small holes at a slight upward angle through the bottom rail of the storm window.

Step 2

Double-hung windows: Attach self-adhesive compressible foam or rubber to the underside of the sash.

Weatherizing Sliding Windows

Treat side-by-side sliding windows as if they were double-hung windows turned 90 degrees, and follow the steps for double-hung windows. However, use metal tension strips instead of self-adhesive foam in the sash track that fits against the sash when the window is shut.

Weatherizing Casement Windows

Attach self-adhesive foam or rubber compression strips on the outside edges of the window stops.

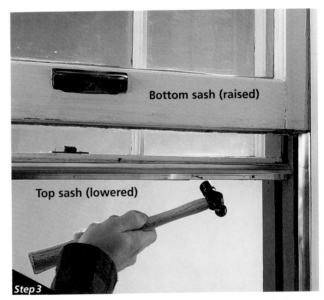

Bottom sash (raised)

Top sash (lowered)

Step 3

Double-hung windows: Use metal V-channel to seal the gap between the top and the bottom sash.

REPLACING SASHES

Replacing a sash is an easy, inexpensive alternative to replacing the entire window. For example, we upgraded the lovely cottage-style window shown here with a sash-replacement kit at half the cost and a fraction of the effort required to install a new window.

Most window manufacturers offer sash replacement kits sized to fit existing windows. These kits are designed to fit existing window frames; all you need to do is remove the window stops, pull out the old sash and install the new one.

Replacement sashes are made of primed wood or wood with a low-maintenance exterior cladding of aluminum or vinyl. Glazing options include single-pane, insulated double-pane and energy-efficient low-e or argon gas-filled panes.

Although most sash-replacement kits are installed in a similar manner, be sure to follow the instructions included with your model. Here are the basic steps involved:

Step 1

A. Before choosing a sash kit, measure the width of the existing window frame between the inside surfaces of the left and right side jambs. Be sure the measuring tape hook is against the jamb, not sitting on the stop molding.

B. Measure the height of the frame from the underside of the head jamb down to the top of the sill.

C. Buy a sash kit to fit these dimensions.

Tools	Materials
• pry bar	• sash-replacement kit
• pliers	• 4d (1½-in.) finishing nails
• putty knife	• wood putty
• hammer	
• nailset	

Step 2

Use a thin pry bar to remove the interior stops from the jambs. If you plan to reuse the stops, work carefully.

Step 3

A. If the sash operates on a rope-and-pulley system, cut the ropes on the bottom sash and let the counterbalance weights drop down inside the wall.

B. Lift out the bottom sash. Pry out the parting stop from the side jambs.

C. Cut the ropes holding the upper sash and lift it out. Remove the pulleys from the jambs.

D. If the sash rides in aluminum tracks, raise the bottom sash and lower the upper sash. Carefully slip the pry bar behind the aluminum window tracks at the top and bottom and lever them away from the jambs.

E. Grab both sashes and tug; they will slip out with the two aluminum side tracks intact.

Step 3

Lever the aluminum window tracks away from the jambs and pull the sashes out of the window frame.

Step 4

A. With a pair of pliers, pull the wooden parting stop from the head jamb.

B. Scrape the jamb smooth with a putty knife.

C. Nail the metal mounting clips to each side jamb. Space the clips as specified in the instructions.

D. Install the new jamb liners by holding them in position, then firmly pushing them onto the clips until they snap into place.

E. Nail the new wood parting strip to the head jamb.

Step 4

Hold the new jamb liner in position and firmly press it onto the metal mounting clips.

Step 5

A. Set the bottom edge of the upper sash between the jamb liners. Insert its pivot pins into the grooves nearest the exterior of the house; be sure the pins are above the clutch assemblies.

Step 5

After installing the upper sash, slip the bottom sash between the two vinyl jamb liners and tilt it into place.

B. Swing up the top of the sash, depress the jamb liners and press the sash into place. Slide the sash down until the pivot pins engage the clutches.

C. Slip the bottom sash between the jamb liners. Set its pivot pins into the grooves nearest the interior. Tilt it into place.

Step 6

A. Refasten the interior stops to the side jambs with finishing nails. Set the nails and fill the holes with putty.

B. Test the sashes to make sure they slide smoothly and lock securely.

Before plastic miniblinds, windows were often covered by handsome wooden shutters that could be opened for light and an outside view or closed for privacy. Today, wooden shutters have been rediscovered by people who are looking for traditional and practical window treatments.

Ready-made hinge-mounted shutters are inexpensive, available with either fixed or movable slats and easy to install on virtually any window.

Step 1

A. Measure the window dimensions and purchase a pair of ready-made shutters. If the exact size isn't available, select shutters that are slightly larger. The shutters should cover half the height of the window. On double-hung windows, they should reach (but not extend past) the top of the lower sash.

Tools
- tape measure
- power miter saw, radial arm saw or table saw
- jointer, belt sander or hand plane
- pencil compass
- screwdriver
- narrow paintbrush

Materials
- 2 pairs ready-made operable-louver shutters
- tape
- ⅛-in. shims
- 120-grit sandpaper
- 2½-in. nonmortising hinges (8)
- screws
- paint or varnish
- decorative brass latch

B. Trim the shutters to the correct height with a power miter saw, radial arm saw or table saw. If you're removing ¾ in. or less, take it all off the bottom of the shutters. If you need to remove more, take half off the top and half off the bottom.

Step 2

A. Make sure the window frame is square before installing the shutters. Tape two shutters together and stand them in the window opening with the left-hand shutter touching the left jamb. Be sure the bottoms of the shutters are flat on the window stool (the flat horizontal molding that rests on the sill).

B. If there's no gap between the jamb and the shutter, that side is square. Tape the other two shutters together and check the right side the same way.

C. If the window is out of square, taper the shutters to accommodate the variance. Adjust a pencil compass to the widest part of the gap. Hold the pivot point against the jamb and slide the compass down from top to bottom of the shutter, marking a corresponding line.

D. Use a jointer, belt sander or hand plane to trim the shutter to the pencil line. Test-fit the shutter in the window opening.

E. If necessary, trim the shutter again until it fits properly.

F. Repeat step 2 for the shutter on the other side, if necessary.

Step 3

A. Position all four shutters in the window and create clearance spaces by putting ⅛-in.-thick shims beneath them and along both sides.

B. Check for uniform ⅛-in. spaces. If necessary, trim the shutters to fit.

C. Lightly sand each shutter with 120-grit sandpaper.

D. Paint, stain or varnish the shutters. Use a narrow brush to reach between the louvers.

Step 4

A. Join each pair of shutters with two 2½-in. nonmortising hinges, screwing them directly to the edges of the shutters. Position each hinge so that its barrel (the part that holds the pin) is on the inside of the shutters facing the window. The shutters should fold outward and swing away from the sash.

B. Attach two hinges to the shutter edges that abut the side jambs. Position the hinge barrels to face out into the room. Hold one pair of shutters in the window opening and drive screws into the side jamb to fasten them. Hang the remaining pair the same way.

C. Close both shutters and check for an even gap where they join in the middle. If necessary, shim behind the jamb hinge to create a uniform gap.

D. Attach a small brass latch to the two middle shutters to hold them closed and add visual interest.

Scribe the shutters and trim along the line to fit out-of-square window frames.

Stand the shutters in position, shim them, and check for uniform spacing.

With the shutter resting on a shim, screw the hinges to the side jamb.

GLASS BLOCK WINDOW

Tools
- reciprocating saw fitted with a metal-cutting blade
- flat pry bar
- hacksaw
- caulking gun

Materials
- 30 8 x 8 glass blocks
- 2 glass block installation kits
- 1½-in. drywall screws
- rubbing alcohol
- silicone adhesive

Glass block offers a stylish way to create windows or partitions that add the right amount of light and privacy to any room. Today this classic look is experiencing a renaissance, and innovative new methods are making glass block quicker and easier than ever to install.

Glass block is durable, energy-efficient, easy to clean and versatile enough to look great on both exterior and interior walls. It also comes in a variety of styles that can provide just the right amount of light transmission and visibility. Clear glass blocks transmit the most light, while translucent frosted blocks offer maximum privacy. In addition to the familiar 4-in.-thick, 8 × 8 size, glass blocks are also available in 6 × 6 in. and 12 × 12 in. dimensions, and a 3-in. thickness.

For this window replacement project we selected a glass block pattern with crisscrossing horizontal and vertical flutes that offer privacy, yet still allow plenty of natural light to shine through—an important consideration in this small bathroom. (If you're replacing a window that's the only source of ventilation in a bathroom, you'll also need to install a ceiling vent fan to prevent moisture and mildew accumulation.)

We also used a mortarless glass block installation kit here. With the kit, we simply set the blocks in a plastic channel, separate them with vertical and horizontal spacer strips and seal the joints with silicone adhesive. Each kit has enough material to install twenty 8 × 8-in. glass blocks.

Step 1

Use a reciprocating saw with a metal-cutting blade to slice through any nails driven between the jambs and the studs.

Step 1

Wearing gloves and eye protection, go outside and use a flat pry bar to detach the old window from the side of the house.

Step 1

A. Inside the house, pry off the interior casing from around the old window.

B. Use a reciprocating saw fitted with a metal-cutting blade to slice through any nails that have been driven through the jambs and into the studs.

C. Wearing gloves and eye protection, go outside and pry the window from the house, using a flat pry bar.

Once you've detached it from the house, pass the window through to an assistant inside the house.

Step 2

A. Measure the rough opening to determine if its dimensions are the right size for a course of whole blocks, both vertically and horizontally. (You can't cut glass block to fit the opening.) Calculate the room

LIGHTING UP YOUR HOME

Step 3

Cut the four plastic channel pieces to fit the rough opening. Screw them into place, then bore weep holes in the lower outside flange.

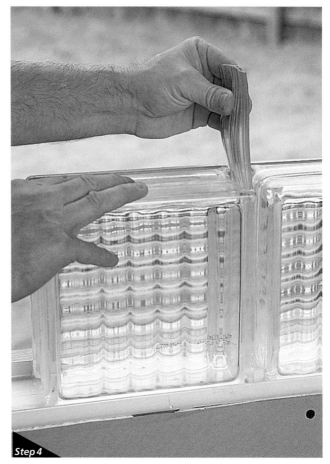

Step 4

Cut lengths of vertical plastic spacer strip the height of the blocks. Hold a strip next to the last block you laid, then slide a new block into place and push the two blocks together.

needed for the spacer strips and plastic channel, as well as the blocks.

B. If the opening can't accommodate a whole course of blocks, reduce it by adding framing to the sides, top or bottom, as needed.

(Reducing the opening is almost always easier than enlarging it, which often requires installing a new header and rough sill.)

Step 3

A. Use a hacksaw to cut the plastic channel so it will fit around the inside of the rough opening.

B. Cut out a section of the upper part of the plastic channel so you'll be able to slide in the last row of blocks. Save the cut-off piece of the channel

(you'll glue it back in place in the last step).

C. Attach the four channel pieces to the rough opening, using 1½-in. drywall screws.

D. Bore ⅛-in.-dia. weep holes in the lower, outer flange.

Step 4

A. To set the first block, press it down into the sill channel and slide it toward the corner until it fits tightly into the side-jamb channel.

B. Cut a vertical length of flexible spacer strip, hold it beside the first block, and slide the second block into position. Push the two blocks together.

C. Repeat this procedure for the

remaining blocks in the first course, inserting a vertical spacer strip between each block. Don't use spacers between the blocks and the channel.

Step 5

A. Lay a flexible spacer strip along the top of the first course. If it won't lie flat, soften it with a heat gun or blow-dryer.

B. Install the second course the same way as the first.

C. Continue in this manner until you reach the top course.

D. Insert the top course of blocks through the notch you cut in the head channel and slide them into position.

E. Insert the vertical spacer strips between the blocks, as in the previous rows.

F. Once all the blocks are installed, carefully check each spacer strip. If any are wrinkled or out of alignment, force them into place with a putty knife.

Step 6

A. Clean both sides of the blocks thoroughly with rubbing alcohol.

B. Place the cartridge of silicone adhesive into a caulking gun. Use the caulking gun to fill all the horizontal joints on the outside of the window with silicone adhesive.

C. Continue by filling all the vertical joints on the outside of the window.

D. Use the spoonlike smoothing tool that comes with the kit to force the silicone into the joints.

E. Immediately remove any excess adhesive.

Set a horizontal length of spacer strip across the top of the first course of blocks. Press it flat, softening it with a heat gun or a blow-dryer, if necessary.

Step 7

A. Fill and smooth the joints on the inside of the window, as above.

B. Use silicone adhesive to secure the piece of flange that you cut off the head channel (in Step 3) back into place.

Insert the top course of blocks through the notch you cut in the head channel. Slide the blocks into place, separating them with the vertical spacer strips. Once all the blocks are in place, check each spacer strip and correct any misalignments.

Fill all the joints between the glass blocks on the inside of the window with silicone adhesive.

TUBULAR SKYLIGHT

Until recently, if you wanted to add natural light to a dark room, your only option was a conventional skylight, but these units are energy-inefficient, expensive and difficult to install. However, now there are new tubular skylights that literally "pipe" in the sun, while minimizing the effort, expense and energy loss associated with conventional skylights.

A tubular skylight has a clear rooftop collector dome that captures light and channels it down a ductlike tube. The highly reflective interior of the tube directs the light through the attic to a diffuser lens mounted on the ceiling of the living area below.

Because the tube fits between the joists and rafters, you don't have to cut into the structural members of the house. And since it can make turns without losing any light, it's easy to avoid vents, ducts and rafter supports. Finally, there's no drywall or painting work required.

All this makes installing a tubular skylight kit a manageable weekend project—in fact, it may take as little as half a day, depending on your skill level.

Before you buy a tubular skylight, you'll need some information. Check the distance between the ceiling and the roof, and determine whether any turns or offsets will be required in the pipe's path. Some models are able to "grab" sunlight even when their dome isn't facing the sun; this comes in handy if you need to place the dome on the shady side of the roof. When planning the location of the diffuser, check whether your ceiling joists and rafters are 16 or 24 in. apart, and choose a spot that falls halfway between two joists.

Although the instructions vary by model, there are three basic tasks involved in installing a tubular skylight: 1) cutting holes in the roof and the ceiling; 2) slipping the pipe in; and 3) installing the collector dome and the diffuser lens. The hardest part is actually shuttling between the attic and the roof. Although you can do most of the work yourself, you'll need a helper to handle the pipe itself. Also, before starting, check the weather forecast—if it starts to rain, you don't want to be caught with a hole in your roof.

Tools
- electric drill
- reciprocating saw or jigsaw
- plumb bob
- screwdriver

Materials
- tubular skylight with installation kit

Step 1

A. Shut off all the electrical circuits in the work area.

B. Mark the center of the diffuser on the ceiling and drill a small hole there. Push a straightened wire clothes hanger into the hole and poke it up through the attic insulation to mark its location.

C. Locate the wire hanger in the attic floor and remove the insulation around it. If the wire isn't centered between two ceiling joists, reposition the center mark and redrill down from the attic.

D. Using a plumb bob, transfer the center mark to the underside of the roof sheathing. Mark and drill a small center hole through the roof.

Step 2

A. Using the adjusted drill hole in the ceiling as the center, measure and mark a hole to fit the outline of the diffuser. Use a reciprocating saw or a jigsaw to cut the hole.

B. On the roof, cut a hole to fit the collector dome.

C. Pry loose the surrounding shingles and center the boot (the one-piece flashing and sleeve that holds the pipe in place) over the hole.

Step 3

A. Push the tube up the ceiling hole from below.

B. In the attic, use screws to secure the bottom of the tube to the adjoining joists.

C. On the roof, fit the white pipe through the metal sleeve. Make sure it fits through the boot snugly.

Step 4

A. Remove the protective film from the reflective surface inside the pipe.

B. Attach the collector dome.

C. Carefully seal the shingles to the boot on the roof, following the manufacturer's instructions.

D. Inside the house, attach the diffuser to the ceiling.

Cut a hole in the ceiling from below to fit the diffuser.

Cut a hole through the roof to fit the collector dome.

Inside the house, push the pipe up through the ceiling.

On the roof, top the pipe with the clear light-collector dome.

LIGHTING UP YOUR HOME

Renewing Doors & Entries

∽∾

Create a dramatic

first impression and

add value to your

home—without

breaking your budget.

∽∾

Renewing Doors & Entries

QUICK REFERENCE		
DOOR UPGRADES	*Weatherizing Doors*	*page 86*
	Security Lock	*page 88*
	Securing a Door	*page 89*
NEW DOORS	*Grand Entrance*	*page 90*
	Storm Door	*page 94*
	Classic Screen Door	*page 96*
	Bifold Closet Doors	*page 98*

When it comes to doors, first impressions mean a lot. Updating a door, whether by replacing it completely or simply by upgrading it, can not only improve the appearance of your home, but also make it considerably safer and more energy efficient, as well.

The projects in this chapter present a range of ways to update your doors in just one weekend. They include installing storm and screen doors, upgrading and weatherizing doors and installing bifold closet doors.

Door installation projects require familiarity with relatively advanced carpentry skills and construction techniques. Before starting a project, read the instructions through to ensure that you have all the tools, materials and skills you'll need for the job. If necessary, ask a friend or neighbor to lend a hand with positioning and installing new doors.

Door Upgrades

Entry doors are designed to last for many years, so before you decide to replace an old entry door, consider how you might improve its performance by weatherizing it or upgrading its security features.

Weatherstripping, caulking and replacing a threshold can greatly improve the energy efficiency of an older exterior door. Although these upgrades require only a small amount of time and minimal carpentry skills, they can have a big payoff: fewer drafts and far lower utility bills.

The other simple door improvements shown here—installing a security lock and securing a door frame—are effective ways to make your home safer and to help prevent break-ins.

New Doors

The first project in this section shows how you can dramatically improve the appearance of an ordinary entrance with a new door and lightweight architectural millwork. This project requires some precision, good carpentry skills and familiarity with power tools.

The next project—replacing a drafty old storm door with a new model—can make a big difference in your heating bill and give your entryway a fresh look as well. Today's storm doors are far more energy-efficient than older models and are available in a wide range of styles.

If you have a vintage house and would like your entry to have the same classic look, consider the next project—a reproduction antique wood screen door. Many antique door designs are now available in kits that offer a rewarding weekend project for an experienced do-it-yourselfer.

Although they're more likely to be overlooked, interior doors can also benefit from an upgrade. For example, bifold doors are a stylish and practical replacement for an old set of sliding closet doors. The two-paneled doors shown here swing open on a pivot, doubling your access to the closet.

WEATHERIZING DOORS

In most homes, a primary area of heat loss is around the entry door—and the weatherstripping around it requires regular maintenance, because it's under constant stress.

Weatherizing an entry door involves adding weatherstripping around the jambs and replacing the threshold. If possible, use only metal weatherstripping products, especially around the jambs—they're more durable than self-adhesive products. If you need a flexible weatherstripping, select a product made of neoprene rubber, rather than foam. A new threshold is one way to further weatherize your door and cut down on drafts. As a rule, you should replace door thresholds or threshold inserts as soon as they begin to show signs of wear.

Weatherstripping a Door
Step 1
A. Cut two pieces of V-channel (metal tension) weatherstripping, one the full height of the door and the other the full width at the top.

B. Use wire brads to tack the weatherstripping to the door jambs and the header on the interior side of the door stops. Attach them from the top down to prevent buckling.

C. Flare out the tension strips with a putty knife to fill the gaps between the jambs and the door when the door is closed (pry gently and slowly).

Tools
- putty knife
- tack hammer
- screwdriver
- backsaw
- flat pry bar
- chisel
- mallet
- tape measure
- drill

Materials
- V-channel (metal tension) weatherstripping
- reinforced felt strips
- door sweep
- nails or brads
- caulk
- new threshold & insert

Weatherstripping: Attach reinforced felt strips to the door stop.

Weatherstripping: Attach a new door sweep.

Step 2

A. Use nails or brads to attach reinforced felt strips to the edge of the door stop on the exterior side. (When the door is closed, the felt edge should create a tight-fitting seal.)

B. Drive the fasteners only until they're flush with the surface of the reinforcing spine—driving them too far may lead to damage and buckling.

Step 3

A. Attach a new door sweep to the bottom of the door on the interior side. If the floor in your entry area is uneven, a felt or bristle door sweep is the best choice.

B. Lightly screw the door sweep into place; test the door swing to make sure there's enough clearance, then permanently tighten the screws.

Replacing a Threshold
Step 1

A. Cut the old wood threshold in two, using a backsaw. Pry out the pieces and clean the debris from the sill area below the threshold.

B. Note which edge of the threshold is more steeply beveled. Install the new threshold in the same way.

Step 2

A. Measure the opening for the new threshold. Trim it to fit, using the old threshold as a template.

B. If the profile of the new threshold is different from the old one, trace the new profile onto the bottoms of the door jamb and stops. Chisel the jamb to fit.

Step 3

A. Apply caulk to the sill.

B. Position the new threshold, pressing it into the caulk.

C. Drive the screws provided with the threshold through the pre-drilled holes in the center channel and into the sill.

D. Install the threshold insert according to the instructions.

Patio Doors

Use rubber compression strips to seal the channels in the patio door jambs, where the movable panels fit when closed.

Install a patio door insulator kit (similar to the plastic sheeting kits used for windows) on the interior side of the door.

Garage Doors

If the old door sweep is in poor condition, attach a new rubber sweep to the lower outside edge of the garage door.

Check the door jambs for drafts and add weatherstripping, if needed.

SECURITY LOCK

Deadbolt security locks have long bolts that extend into the door jamb. Because they're an effective deterrent against intruders, installing one on an entry door may qualify you for a reduction in your homeowner's insurance rate.

At one time, double-cylinder deadbolt locks keyed on both sides were often used in doors with sidelights or other glass elements to prevent break-ins through the glass. However, these locks are no longer allowed by code and should be replaced. In an emergency, such as a house fire, double-cylinder keyed locks can trap people inside the house if they can't find the key.

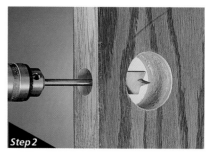

Bore a cylinder hole through the door, then a latchbolt hole into the side edge.

Insert the latchbolt, then insert the lock pieces and screw them together.

Step 1

A. Measure the door to determine the proper height of the lock on the door. Tape the cardboard template that comes with the lockset onto the door at that height.

B. Use a nail or an awl to mark the centerpoints of the cylinder and the latchbolt holes on the door, placing them according to the lock template.

Step 2

A. Use a hole saw and drill to bore the cylinder hole into the door. To avoid splintering the wood, drill through one side until the hole saw pilot bit (the mandrel) just comes out the other side. Remove the hole saw and complete the hole from the opposite side of the door.

B. Use a spade bit and drill to bore the latchbolt hole from the edge of the door into the cylinder hole. Keep the drill perpendicular to the door edge while drilling.

Step 3

A. Insert the latchbolt into the edge hole.

B. Insert the lock tailpiece and the connecting screws through the latchbolt mechanism and screw the cylinders together.

Step 4

A. Close the door to find the point where the latchbolt meets the door jamb; this is the position of the strike plate. Score the outline of the strike plate on the door frame with a utility knife, using the hardware as a template.

B. Chisel around the outline of the mortise, holding the tool bevel-side in. Tap the butt end lightly with a mallet until the chisel reaches the right depth.

C. Chisel a series of parallel cuts ¼-in. apart over the mortise, hold-

ing the tool at a 45-degree angle. Lever out the waste, pointing the tool downward at a low angle, with the beveled edge toward the wood.

D. Use a spade bit to bore the latchbolt hole into the center of the mortise.

E. Secure the strike plate to the mortise, using the retainer screws provided with the lockset. The screws should be at least 3 in. long so they extend through the jamb and into the trimmer stud.

Tools
- tape measure
- awl
- utility knife
- mallet
- lockset drill kit with hole saw & spade bit
- drill
- chisel

Materials
- security lock (deadbolt) kit

SECURING A DOOR

Drafts aren't the only thing that can sneak in through an unsecured door frame—a loose frame also allows intruders to pry their way in more easily. However, a few simple steps can ensure that your door is not only weatherized, but securely attached to the house.

Step 1

A. First, test the frame to find out if it needs additional support. Cut a 2×4 about 1 in. longer than the width of the door. Wedge the board between the jambs near the lockset.

B. Check the door frame. If it flexes more than ¼ in., it should be secured more tightly—proceed to step 2.

Step 2

A. Remove the interior jamb casing to reveal the shims between the jambs and the framing members.

Measure the gap between them.

B. Cut plywood shims to the thickness of the gap between the jambs and the framing members. Insert the plywood between the existing shims.

Step 3

A. Drive casing nails through the jambs and the shims into the framing members.

B. Set the nailheads and reattach the door casing.

More Tips for Securing Doors

For added security, you can also incorporate these security measures into your entry door:

• Add metal sleeves to the edges of the door around the lockset and the deadbolt. This will help keep anyone from kicking the door in. Make sure the sleeves are the correct thickness for your door.

• Add heavy-duty strike plates to reinforce the door and the locks. This will help prevent kick-ins, jimmying and prying. Select a strike plate that has a flange that protects the lockset from being pried loose.

• Install a wide-angle viewer in entry doors. To do this, drill an eye-level hole through the door, the same diameter as the shaft of the viewer. Insert the shaft so that the attached eyepiece is flush against the door. Screw the exterior eyepiece onto the shaft.

Tools
• tape measure
• circular saw
• hammer
• nailset

Materials
• 2x4
• plywood shims
• 10d (3-in.) casing nails

Step 1

Wedge a 2×4 between the door jambs and check the frame.

Step 3

Nail through the jambs, the new shims and the door frame.

GRAND ENTRANCE

A handsome, well-designed front door creates a favorable first impression of your home. Yet, most front entries lack style or personality. As you'll see here, it can be easy to transform an ordinary door into an elegant entryway in one weekend.

Like many front doors, this one had no decorative trim or accents. Also, since the door was only fitted with two tiny lights, the foyer was dark and shadowy. The challenge was to create a brighter, wider and more stylish entry, without enlarging the existing opening.

We pursued that goal with a three-step strategy. First, we replaced the old door with a steel model with two large lights (steps 1 to 3). Since the original wooden frame was good, we replaced just the door, using a replacement door designed for easy installation into an existing door frame.

Second, we trimmed the exterior

Tools
- screwdriver
- portable circular saw
- cordless drill/driver
- straightedge
- hacksaw
- hammer
- caulk gun

Materials
- new steel door & hardware
- new storm door & hardware
- lockset
- architectural millwork: crosshead pediment, fluted columns, plinth blocks
- 10d (3-in.) galvanized finishing nails
- roofing nails
- urethane adhesive
- exterior-grade wood putty
- caulk

of the door with a pair of fluted columns and a crosshead pediment (steps 4 and 5). The new trim visually extended the doorway from 3 ft. to 5 ft. wide.

Instead of wood trim, which requires regular upkeep, we used architectural millwork—a high-quality, low-maintenance alternative. Molded from durable high-density urethane foam, it comes primed white and is impervious to rot, insects, moisture, cracking and splitting. Best of all, it's easy to install and looks like handcrafted wood molding, even up close.

Third, we finished the entryway by adding an attractive aluminum storm door to protect the entry door and increase its energy efficiency (step 6). This is the easiest part of the job; it took us about an hour.

Remove the wood threshold from the sill to create a flush surface for the new door.

Step 1

Select a replacement door that comes prehung in a steel frame and has a threshold designed to fit into the existing wood frame.

A. Carefully pry off the casing from around the inside of the door.

B. Unscrew the hinges from the side jambs and remove the old door—have a helper hold the unit as you remove the last few screws.

C. Unscrew the old strike plate from the side jamb.

Step 2

A. Remove the adjustable wood strip from the original threshold to create a flush surface for installing the new door. If there's no adjustable part, chisel the surface flush or cut out the whole sill.

B. Sweep the sill clean and apply two thick beads of caulk where the new threshold will go.

Step 3

A. Set the threshold of the new door onto the sill and tilt the door into the opening. Make sure its steel frame fits snugly around the doorway opening.

B. Make sure the frame is square and the door is plumb.

C. Temporarily secure the door by driving roofing nails through the predrilled holes in the steel frame and into the trimmer studs on each side of the opening.

D. Swing open the door. Use a cordless drill/driver to drive long "security" screws through the sides and top of the steel door frame. Don't overtighten these screws; this could distort the frame.

E. Install a lockset (see **Security Lock**, page 88).

Tilt the prehung replacement door into position. Make sure its frame fits snugly around the doorway opening.

Drive roofing nails through the holes in the frame and into the trimmer studs on each side of the opening.

Cut the fluted columns to length; place one under each end of the pediment. Nail in place.

Attach a plinth block to the base of each fluted column, using urethane adhesive and nails.

F. Nail on the magnetic weatherstripping that comes with the door.

Step 4

The easiest way to install the columns and pediment is to nail them over the siding. However, if you cut back the siding and nail the trim to the sheathing, it will appear to be original. Here's how to do it:

A. Tack a straightedge board to the house to use as a guide.

B. Run a circular saw along the guide, cutting only through the siding.

C. Pry off the severed siding pieces and strip away the housewrap or building felt to expose the sheathing.

Step 5

A. Apply a bead of urethane adhesive to the back of the pediment.

B. Press the pediment into position above the door. Fasten it with eight 10d galvanized finishing nails.

C. Cut the fluted columns to size and install them in the same manner.

Use a hacksaw to trim off the bottom end of the combination hinge/mounting flange on the door.

Press the door sweep onto the bottom of the door. Tighten it against the threshold after installing the door.

D. Apply urethane adhesive to the back of the plinth blocks. Nail one to the bottom of each column.

E. Set all the nailheads and fill the holes with exterior-grade putty.

Step 6

A. Screw the combination hinge/mounting flange to the storm door.

B. Use a hacksaw to trim the flange to fit the bottom of the storm door.

C. Insert the flexible rubber fin into the slot in the expander door sweep, and slip the sweep onto the bottom of the storm door.

D. Set the storm door into the opening; have a helper hold it while you drive screws through the mounting flange and into the existing wood brick mold.

E. Install the latch-side and head-mounting flanges the same way. You can hide the mounting screws by snapping on the plastic cover strips.

F. Finish by installing the door closer and the lockset included with the storm door.

Secure the storm door by driving screws through the mounting flange and into the wood brick mold.

STORM DOOR

One of the most effective ways to immediately improve both the appearance and the performance of an entry door is to replace the storm door.

Today's storm doors are attractive, solidly constructed designs that offer both beauty and utility. The new models come in a wide range of styles and offer excellent energy efficiency.

When buying a storm door, look for a unit that has a solid inner core and seamless outer shell construction. To get a good fit, carefully measure the dimensions of your door opening, rather than your existing storm door. And finally, remember to choose a storm door that opens on the same side as your entry door.

Step 1

A. Before buying a storm door, measure the door opening. Take the height and width of the inside edges of the brick molding on the entry door. Select a door that fits these dimensions.

B. Because entry thresholds are slanted, you'll need to cut the frame of the storm door to match the angle of the threshold. To determine the angle of the cut, measure from the outer threshold to the the top of the door opening at the edge of the brick molding (A), and at the front edge of the entry door stop (B), as shown.

C. Subtract ⅛ in. from measurements A and B to allow for adjustments when the door is installed.

D. Measuring from the top of the storm door frame, mark the position of the adjusted points A and B on the corner bead.

Tools
- tape measure
- pencil
- hacksaw
- hammer
- drill
- screwdriver

Materials
- storm door unit
- wood spacer strips
- 4d (1½-in.) casing nails

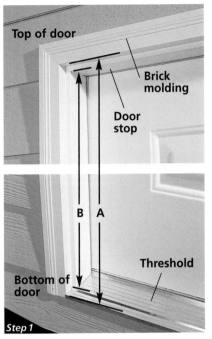

Take the outside (A) and the inside (B) dimensions of the door opening.

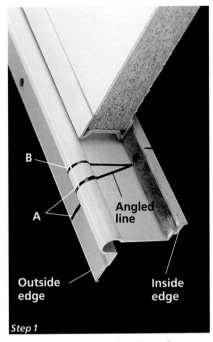

Draw a line from point A on the corner bead to point B on the inside edge.

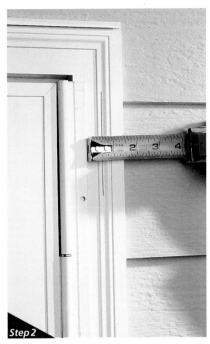

Measure the gap between the line and the hinge side of the door frame.

E. Draw a line from point A to the outside edge of the frame and from point B to the inside edge, as shown. Draw an angled line from point A on the corner bead to point B on the inside edge.

F. Use a hacksaw to cut down through the bottom of the storm door frame, following the angled line. Hold the hacksaw at the same slant as the angled line for a smooth, straight cut.

Step 2

A. Position the storm door in the opening and pull the frame tightly against the brick molding on the hinge side of the storm door.

B. Draw a reference line onto the brick molding, following the edge of the storm door frame.

C. Push the storm door tightly against the brick molding on the latch side. Measure the gap between the reference line and the hinge side of the door frame.

D. If the distance is greater than ⅜ in., install spacer strips to ensure the door will fit snugly: Remove the door, and nail thin strips of wood to the inside of the brick molding where the storm door's hinges are located. The thickness of the wood strips should be ⅛ in. less than the width of the gap.

Step 3

A. Attach the sweep to the bottom of the door. Replace the storm door and push it tightly against brick molding on the hinge side.

B. Drill pilot holes through the hinge side frame of the storm door and into the brick molding.

C. Secure the frame with mounting screws spaced every 12 in.

Step 4

A. Remove any spacer clips that are holding the frame to the storm door. Close the storm door, drill pilot holes and attach the latch side frame to the brick molding. Use a coin to maintain an even gap between the storm door and its frame.

B. Center the top piece of the storm door frame on top of the side frames. Drill pilot holes and screw the top piece to the brick molding.

Step 5

A. Adjust the height of the bottom sweep so it brushes the top of the sill lightly.

B. Attach locks and latch hardware as directed by the manufacturer.

CLASSIC SCREEN DOOR

Although wood screen doors are no longer as common as they once were, they still offer a graceful charm that aluminum screen doors simply can't match. This handcrafted door, which was installed in just three days, does more than just keep out bugs and let in fresh air—its graceful accents also complement the look of this vintage home.

Reproduction wood screen doors such as this one are available in ready-to-assemble kits in a wide range of styles, and you're sure to find one that will perfectly complement your home. Each design has different details that you'll need to assemble according to the manufacturer's instructions, but the basic installation method is the same. Here's how to assemble and install this classic screen door:

Step 1

A. Before ordering a screen door kit, carefully measure the top, middle and bottom of the door opening. Also measure the height from the head jamb (the horizontal part of the door frame at the top) to the threshold along each side jamb.

B. If the opening isn't exactly square, order a door to match the larger dimensions and trim it to fit.

Step 2

A. Spread weatherproof glue liberally onto the joints of the precut door frame.

B. Draw each joint closed with two pipe clamps. Place one clamp above the door and one below the door to distribute the pressure evenly and prevent bowing.

C. Glue and clamp the spandrel (middle) rail together.

Step 3

A. Miter-cut the parts of the screen frame to length and screw

Tools
- four 4-ft. pipe clamps
- caulking gun
- spline roller
- hammer
- pry bar
- plane or belt sander
- screwdriver

Materials
- precut screen door kit
- weatherproof glue
- construction adhesive
- ⅛-in.-dia. rubber spline (20 lin. ft.)
- 2d, 4d galvanized finishing nails
- fiberglass or aluminum screening
- 3-in. full-surface hinges (3)
- turnbuttons (10)
- galvanized screws
- cedar-shingle shims
- pneumatic door closer

Draw the joints in the door frame closed with two pipe clamps.

Press the spline into the groove with the concave wheel of a spline roller.

Shim the door until it's exactly centered in the door frame opening.

them together. Paint or stain them.

B. Trim the the inside of the door frame with ¼-in. lattice strips, using 2d finishing nails.

C. Fasten the spandrel rail and the quarter-circle brackets to the inside of the door frame with construction adhesive and 4d finishing nails.

Step 4

A. Cut the screening 8 in. wider and longer than the screen opening; a big overlap makes it easy to handle.

B. Clamp one end to the screen frame, then pull the other end taut.

C. Use the convex wheel of a spline roller to gently press the screening into the grooves in the back of the frame. Flip the tool over and use its concave wheel to push in the rubber spline that secures the screening.

Step 5

A. Pry off the old stops from around the inside of the doorway.

B. Place the screen door in the opening and check its fit. Plane or belt-sand the edges and ends to allow a ³/₁₆-in.-wide space around the entire unit.

C. Paint or stain the door.

Step 6

A. Use cedar-shingle shims to hold the door centered in the opening. To avoid cutting mortises, hang the door in the opening with three full-surface hinges.

B. Attach the hinges directly to the door and to the outside casing, using galvanized screws.

C. Use the turnbuttons to secure the screen frame to the door. On the inside, nail new stops to the side and head jambs.

D. Install a lockset and attach a pneumatic door closer. Turn the closer's valve screw to adjust the tension until the door closes and latches securely without slamming.

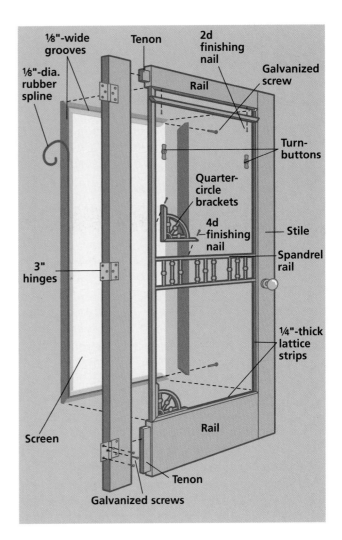

BIFOLD CLOSET DOORS

Raised-panel bifold doors such as those shown at left are a stylish replacement for old-fashioned sliders. These doors are a convenient addition to any closet, since they provide easy access to the entire storage area without requiring too much clearance room.

Replacing or upgrading a set of bifold doors is an easy task. The model we install here operates by means of six posts: a top and bottom pivot post on each jamb-side door and a top guiding post on each lead door. In addition, you need to install a track at the header and a bottom bracket at each jamb.

Tools
- tape measure
- screwdriver
- plane
- circular saw

Materials
- pair of bifold doors with hinges & mounting hardware
- screws

Step 1

A. Measure the width of the closet opening. Subtract ⅞ in. from that measurement to allow clearance between the doors.

B. Divide this total by two to determine the width of each bifold pair.

C. Purchase a pair of bifold doors to fit the measurement. If your doorway isn't a standard size, you have two options. You can either order the doors too wide and plane them to your measurements, or order them too narrow and reduce the size of the closet opening (see step 3A).

Step 2

A. Pop the old doors out of the sliding track by simultaneously lifting and pulling inward. If necessary, unscrew the roller hardware from the upper inside surface of each door.

B. Unscrew the metal door track from the header.

C. Remove the floor guide by backing out the screws and separating the guide into two pieces.

Step 3

A. If necessary, adjust the size of the door to fit the dimensions of the opening.

If the doors are too large, plane the door to fit. If they're too small, reduce the width of the doorway by nailing a 1×4 to each side jamb and attaching ¾-in. cove molding to hide the filler strips.

B. Fasten the overhead door track for the new doors by driving 1½-in.-long screws up into the header. Position the tracks so that the installed doors will be ¾ in. back from the outside of the casing.

C. If the closet opening has a valance, screw a 2×2 mounting strip to the back of the valance. Position it so the door track is flush with the

Step 3

Screw the jamb bracket to the side of the opening. The bracket supports the pivot post on the bottom of the door.

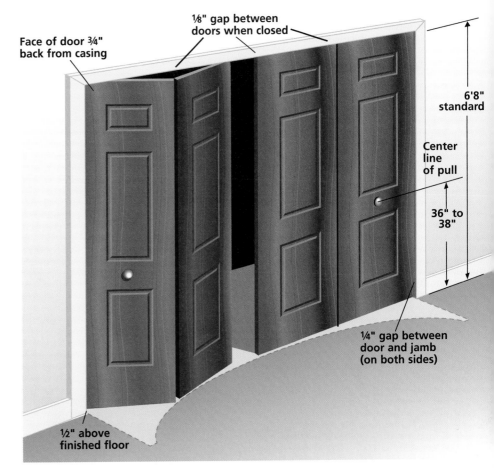

Face of door ¾" back from casing

⅛" gap between doors when closed

6'8" standard

Center line of pull

36" to 38"

¼" gap between door and jamb (on both sides)

½" above finished floor

valance, then drive the screws up through the track and into the 2×2.

D. Fasten an L-shaped jamb bracket to each side jamb. Be sure the center of the bracket aligns precisely with the center of the overhead door track.

Step 4

A. Lay the doors facedown and attach the hinges. Each pair of doors requires three hinges.

B. Check the height of the doors in the opening. They're designed to fit a standard 6 ft. 8 in. opening, but if the floor is carpeted or tiled, you may need to trim them.

C. Screw a pivot post to the top and bottom of the two doors. Position each steel post bracket exactly ⅝ in. from the door edge.

D. Attach a guide to the top of the doors where they meet in the center.

Step 5

A. Fold one pair of doors closed, lift it into position and insert its two top pivots into the track. Slip the bottom pivot post into the jamb bracket.

B. Repeat this process for the other pair of doors.

Step 4

Screw one pivot post to the doors at the side jambs.

C. Close both doors and check for equal spacing along the side jambs and down the center.

D. Adjust the door height by turning the bottom pivot clockwise to lower it or counterclockwise to raise it.

E. Align the door vertically by loosening the screw in the top pivot point guide and sliding it left or right.

The bottom pivot can be positioned anywhere along the length of the pivot angle for an additional vertical adjustment.

Adding Shelving & Storage

Discover how
these ingenious new
ideas can add
welcome storage
space to your home.

Adding Shelving & Storage

	QUICK REFERENCE	
DISPLAY	*Mantel Shelf*	*page 104*
SHELVING	*Bin-&-Shelving Units*	*page 106*
	Wall Boxes	*page 108*
RECESSED	*Picture Frame Shelves*	*page 110*
SHELVING	*Kitchen Wine Rack*	*page 112*
	Stairway Pantry	*page 114*
WALL UNITS	*Wall-to-Wall Bookcases*	*page 116*
	Entertainment Center	*page 118*
	Floor-to-Ceiling Shelves	*page 122*
SHELF ADD-ONS	*Lighting a Wall Unit*	*page 126*
	Glide-Out Shelves	*page 128*

If you think you've exhausted all your home's storage and shelving possibilities, look again. The projects here can help you spot new storage space that may have been hidden along a stairway, inside a wall or above a kitchen cabinet.

The carpentry skills required for these projects range from simple to advanced. Begin with one that's suited to your skill level, and build your confidence before proceeding to the more complicated projects.

Display Shelving

Small ornamental shelves can provide a spot for collectibles, display objects and household items. Mantel shelves and wall boxes are an attractive alternative to traditional shelves and relatively simple to build. The unique design of bin-and-shelving units is both practical and appealing—and the detailed instructions for this project make it ideal for a beginning carpenter.

Recessed Shelving

Recessed shelves make use of the storage space hidden between wall

studs. You simply build a cabinet, insert it into a hole in the wall and add a face frame. The possibilities for recessed shelving are almost limitless—an ordinary wall can become a bookcase, a kitchen soffit can become a wine rack, a basement stairwell can become a pantry.

These projects are affordable and easy to build in a weekend, even for a do-it-yourselfer with relatively little carpentry experience. Just make sure you don't accidentally cut into electrical wires or ductwork when you open up the wall.

Wall Units

The first two projects here, a wall-to-wall bookcase and an entertainment center, are quite simple because they're constructed with stock kitchen cabinets. This approach puts these projects well within the reach of a do-it-yourselfer with average carpentry skills. You simply screw the cabinets

together and attach them to the wall as a unit. The matching moldings give the units a built-in look. If you take care in matching the cabinets to your wall trim, the results can be as impressive as a custom-built unit.

If you have advanced carpentry skills, consider the last project in this section. It describes how to build an impressive floor-to-ceiling wall unit in a weekend or two, for a fraction of the retail cost.

Shelf Add-Ons

The final step in customizing a wall unit is adding the wiring and lighting. By selecting the right light fixtures and concealing the wires, you can transform an ordinary set of shelves into an elegant showcase for your collectibles. Another shelf add-on, glide-out shelves, makes it easier to access the items at the back of a deep cabinet.

MANTEL SHELF

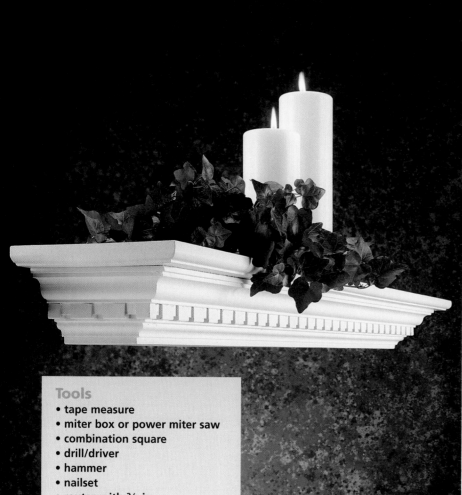

Although this mantel appears to be made from a solid piece of milled hardwood, its looks are deceiving. We used stock moldings to hide a simple support framework, and an antique white paint to disguise the inexpensive poplar lumber. For a natural finish, you could build the mantel from oak, then stain it.

Step 1

A. Cut the 2×4 shelf bottom, 2×2 center supports and 2×2 end supports to size. Miter one end of each support at 45 degrees.

B. Draw lines on the top face of the shelf bottom, 13 and 14½ in. from each end.

C. Position the end supports, drill pilot holes and attach with glue and 2¼ in. screws.

D. Cut the 2×2 ledger to length and test-fit it between the end supports so the back edges of the ledger and bottom are flush.

E. Position the center supports against the ledger along the reference lines. Drill countersunk pilot holes for the screws. Attach the center supports with glue and screws.

Step 2

A. Cut the front crown molding and the two returns to size. Miter the ends at 45 degrees.

B. Position the front crown so the top edge is flush with the top edge of the supports and the lower edge rests against the front edge of the bottom.

C. Drill pilot holes; attach the front crown to the supports and the bottom with wood glue and 4d finishing nails.

D. Attach the two return crown moldings in the same way. Nail through the joints with 2d nails from both directions.

E. Set all the nail heads.

Tools

- tape measure
- miter box or power miter saw
- combination square
- drill/driver
- hammer
- nailset
- router with ⅜-in. roundover bit
- level
- sander
- paintbrush
- miter box

Materials

- 1x8 poplar or oak (6 ft.)
- 2x4 poplar or oak (4 ft.)
- 2x2 poplar or oak (6 ft.)
- ¾ x 3¾-in. crown molding (5 ft.)
- ½ x ⅝-in. dentil molding (5 ft.)
- wood glue
- #8 x 2¼-in. wood screws
- #6 x 1½-in. trim-head screws
- 3½-in. drywall screws
- 2d & 4d finishing nails
- sandpaper
- wood putty
- antique white paint or stain

Step 1

Position the center supports along the ledger, drill pilot holes and fasten.

Attach the front crown molding and the returns to the bottom and supports.

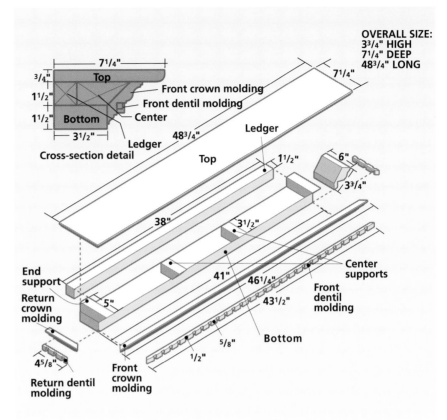

OVERALL SIZE:
3³/₄" HIGH
7¹/₄" DEEP
48³/₄" LONG

Top

Front crown molding
Front dentil molding
Center

Bottom

Ledger

Cross-section detail

Ledger

Top

End support

Return crown molding

Center supports

Front dentil molding

Bottom

Return dentil molding

Front crown molding

Step 3

A. Cut the top to size. Smooth with medium-grit sandpaper.

B. Round both the ends and the front edge with a router fitted with a ³/₈-in. roundover bit set for a ¹/₈-in. shoulder.

C. Place the top facedown. Mark the positions of the supports on the underside. Drill pilot holes; attach the top to the supports with glue and 4d nails. The back edges of the top and supports should be flush. Set the nailheads.

Step 4

A. Cut the front and side dentil molding to size, mitering the intersecting ends at a 45-degree angle. Cut through the "tooth" part of each piece so the pattern will match at the corners.

B. Position the front dentil molding and the two returns on the crown molding. Drill pilot holes and attach with glue and 4d nails, keeping the mitered joints tight. Nail the joints from both directions with 2d nails. Set the nailheads.

Attach the dentil molding to the crown molding, keeping the joints tight.

Step 5

A. Position the ledger on the wall, making sure it's level.

B. Drill pilot holes; attach the ledger to the wall with 3½-in. drywall screws driven into wall studs.

C. Fit the shelf over the ledger. Drill pilot holes for 1½-in. trim-head wood screws through the top and into the ledger.

D. Remove the shelf from the wall. Apply wood putty to all the nail holes. Scrape off any excess putty.

E. Sand the shelf until smooth and finish with paint or stain. Allow it to dry thoroughly.

F. Position the shelf over the ledger. Mount the shelf with 1½-in. trim-head screws driven into the pilot holes.

G. Fill screw holes with wood putty and touch up the finish.

Bin & Shelving Units

Tools

- circular saw
- clamp
- drill
- hammer
- 1/8-in. drill bit with 3/8-in.-dia. counterbore
- small handsaw
- sanding block
- level

Materials

- 3/4-in. medium-density fiberboard (2 ft. x 4 ft.) or
  1x6 lumber (4 ft.)
- 1/4-in. tempered hardboard (2 ft. x 4 ft.) or
  1x8 lumber (3 ft.)
- #8 x 3-in. brass oval-head screws & finishing washers or
  #10 x 3-in. brass oval-head screws & finishing washers
- 3/8-in. dowel
- cotton swabs
- 1 5/8-in. wood screws
- wood glue
- sandpaper
- toggle bolt anchors
- acrylic or latex paint or wood stain & clear acrylic finish

These unique bin-and-shelving units can support a glass or wooden shelf—and you can add or subtract V-sections to adjust the unit to fit the available wall space in a small bathroom. The shelves can also be mounted diagonally on the wall to create a stair-step effect.

If you plan to paint the shelves, you can use medium-density fiberboard (MDF) for the bins and hardboard for the backboard—the surfaces of these materials will accept paint well. If you're using a hardboard backboard, use #8 oval-head screws.

If you prefer a stained wood finish, use 1×6 lumber for the bins and 1×8 lumber for the backboard. If you're using a solid wood backboard, use #10 oval-head screws.

Step 1

A. Cut six shelving pieces from fiberboard or 1×6 lumber. Cut one piece 5½ × 8¼ in. and label it "A" on a piece of tape. Cut five more pieces 5½ × 7½ in. and label them "B" through "F."

B. Position the pieces in order, as shown in photo, placing piece "A" at the far right and working left.

C. Clamp piece "B" to piece "A" at a right angle. Mark the location of two screws on "A," ⅜ in. from the lower edge and 1 in. from each side.

Mark the location of a third screw centered between the first two.

D. To make the pilot holes for the screws, use a counterbore bit. Drill deep enough to create a ¼-in.-deep counterbore in the top section of the pilot hole.

E. Drill pilot screw holes through "A" and into "B." Secure "A" to "B" with 1⅝-in. wood screws.

F. Clamp "C" to "B" at a right angle and join as above. Repeat for "D" through "F."

Step 1

Position the pieces for assembly, with piece A at the far right.

Step 2

Mark the position of the assembly screws on the backboard.

Step 2

A. Lay the V-sections on the front of the backboard, with the upper points flush with the top edge of the backboard. Trace the edges of the V-sections onto the backboard.

B. Cut off the backboard along the lower outline. Draw lines on the front of the backboard showing the location of the wood screws inside the V-sections.

C. Mark the position of three screws along each side of the V-sections, avoiding the lines for the wood screws.

D. Drill holes through the backboard at the new marks, using a ⅛-in. drill bit.

Step 3

A. Place the V-sections front-edge down. Place the backboard front-face down on top of it, with the edges aligned.

B. Keeping the pieces aligned, drill the pilot hole closest to the center V, creating a ¼-in.-deep counterbore. Drive a wood screw through the hole. Recheck the alignment.

C. Drill counterbored pilot holes and drive in the screws at the ends of the unit.

D. Drill counterbored pilot holes and drive in all remaining screws.

Step 4

A. Cut a ½-in. piece of dowel to make plugs for the counterbored screw holes. Bevel one end of each plug by sanding or filing it slightly.

B. Apply wood glue to the inside surface of the holes, using a cotton swab. Tap the plugs into the holes as far as possible with a hammer; the fit should be quite snug.

C. Wipe away any excess glue with a damp cloth. Let the glue dry thoroughly before proceeding.

Step 5

A. Sand the outer edges of the backboard and the edges of the shelves. Cut off the excess plugs with a small handsaw, taking care not to scratch the wood surface.

B. Sand the plugs flush with the surface, using rough sandpaper on a sanding block. Sand the entire unit until smooth.

C. Paint the unit, or apply a stain and clear acrylic finish.

D. Mark the position of mounting screws on the front of the backboard, centered over each V-section and 1 in. down from the top. Drill pilot holes with a ⅛-in. bit.

Step 6

A. Position the shelving on the wall. Tap a small nail partway into the wall through one screw hole.

B. Place a carpenter's level on top of the shelving. With the nail holding it at one end, slide the other end up and down until the unit is level. Use a nail to mark the placement of the screw on that end.

C. Remove the shelf. Drill pilot holes for toggle bolt anchors into the wall at the marks. If there's a stud at a mark, drive a wood screw directly into the stud instead.

D. Place the shelving in position on the wall. Screw it to wall studs (using washers) or follow the manufacturer's instructions for installing the toggle bolt anchors, running each bolt through a finishing washer and into the holes.

WALL BOXES

Tools
- jigsaw or circular saw
- drill
- counterbore drill bit
- sanding block
- nailset
- hammer
- paintbrush

Materials
- ½-in. hardwood, A-A plywood or medium-density fiberboard
- 1x3s
- 1x2 scraps
- wood glue
- 16 x 1½-in. brads
- ¼-in. tempered glass shelves
- ¼-in. x ¾-in. pine or oak molding
- wood filler
- sandpaper
- paint or stain
- #8 wood screws

Wall boxes offer almost endless display possibilities. They can be any size or depth, painted or stained and can be used alone or in groups. You can add glass shelves for an open curio case or create a display ledge by placing the open side against the wall. Other ideas include adding a picture frame molding or hinged shutters to the outside of the box.

Step 1

A. Decide on the dimensions of the wall box. The outside dimensions will be 1 in. higher and wider than the display opening. The depth will be 1¼ in. deeper than the display area, since the back is recessed.

B. Cut the backboard of the box to the exact dimensions of the display opening.

C. Cut the top and bottom of the box, making them as long as the backboard and as deep as the display area plus 1¼ in.

D. Cut the sides the height of the backboard plus two thicknesses of the material you're using, and the same depth as the top and bottom of the box.

Step 2

A. Place the backboard on 1×2 boards to raise it ¾ in. up from the work surface. Apply a bead of wood glue to its top edge. Position the top upright against the glued edge, with the side ends aligned.

B. Secure the top to the backboard, using brads placed 1 in. from the back and side edges of the board. Space the remaining brads at

Step 2

Place the backboard on 1×2s to raise it up. Place the top upright against it.

Step 5

Glue the narrow strip of the mounting rail to the top back of the box.

the top of the box, with the angled edge pointing down, as shown. Anchor the strip with brads driven down through the top.

Step 6

A. Position the wide strip of the mounting rail on the wall, making sure it's level. Point its angled edge up so it will fit under the matching angle on the wall box. Mark the placement on the wall.

B. Use a ⅛-in. drill bit to drill screw holes through the mounting rail and into the wall, at stud locations, if possible. Where there is no wall stud, install plastic toggles into the holes.

C. Secure the rail to the wall with #8 wood screws.

Step 7

A. Mount the wall box onto the mounting rail.

B. Have tempered glass shelves cut by a glazier to fit the display area of the box, less ⅛ in. on the side and back edges. Install the shelves.

4- to 6-in. intervals. Recess the brads with a nailset.

C. Attach the bottom to the backboard in the same way.

Step 3

A. If you're adding a glass shelf, mark its position by aligning the sides and marking lines along the front edges. If you're not adding a shelf, skip to step 3D.

B. Cut molding strips equal to the depth of the display area, less ⅜ in. Sand the ends.

C. Align the molding strips on the marked lines ¼ in. from the front edge. Attach the strips with glue and 1½-in. brads. Recess the brads with a nailset. Fill the holes with wood filler.

D. Attach the sides to the box, using glue and brads driven into the edges of the backboard and the top and bottom pieces.

Step 4

A. Sand the ends of the sides flush with the top of the box, using rough

sandpaper on a sanding block. Sand the top of shelf using medium and fine sandpaper. Repeat for the bottom of the box.

B. Sand the front and back edges. Fill the nail holes and the plywood edges with the wood filler. Sand them smooth.

C. Paint or stain the box.

Step 5

A. On a piece of 1×3 at least 8 in. longer than the box, mark a continuous line along one long side, 1 in. from the edge.

B. Clamp the board at the ends, then use a circular saw or a jigsaw to bevel-cut the board at a 45-degree angle along the long line, angling the blade toward the closer edge.

C. Cross-cut the pieces to a length that equals the width of the back piece.

D. Lightly sand the sharp angled edges of the mounting rail pieces. Glue the narrow strip of the mounting rail to the underside of

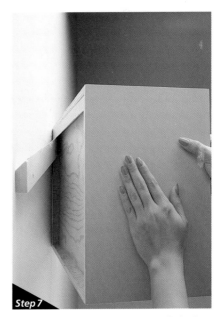

Step 7

Mount the box, fitting the angled edges of the mounting rail pieces together.

PICTURE FRAME SHELVES

Finding more storage space is easy—if you know where to look. Picture frame recessed shelving, for example, is an easy, attractive and versatile way to create built-in shelving inside the walls of your home. This space-saving project simply involves opening a wall, installing a shallow wooden cabinet in the hole and adding shelving and a hardwood face frame.

Step 1

A. Locate the wall studs in the area you want to put the shelves. Cut a small hole in the wall, and use a flashlight to make sure there aren't any plumbing ducts or electrical cables in the wall. If there are, patch the hole and choose another spot.

B. Mark the cutout area on the wall, using a level as a guide. The sides of the cutout should follow the edges of the wall studs, and its height should allow for the thickness of a 2×4 header and sill plate.

C. Use a jigsaw to cut out along the marked lines.

Step 2

A. Cut the center stud at the top and bottom edge of the opening with a reciprocating saw.

B. Fit the saw with a flexible 12-in. blade and cut any fasteners between the cut portion of the stud and the finish layer on the opposite side of the wall.

C. Use a flat pry bar to remove the cut portion of the stud. Take care not to damage the opposite wall.

Step 3

A. Measure between the flanking studs at the top and bottom of the hole. Cut a header and a sill from 2×4 lumber to those measurements.

B. Attach the header and the sill to the cripple (cut) stud and the flanking studs, using 3-in. screws.

Tools
- flashlight
- pencil
- level
- jigsaw
- reciprocating saw with flexible 12-in. blade
- flat pry bar
- drill/driver, bits
- portable drill stand
- pegboard scraps
- pipe clamps
- hammer
- tape measure
- utility knife
- paintbrush

Materials
- wood glue
- 1½-in. finishing nails
- 3-in. finishing nails
- 1½-in. wood screws
- 3-in. wood screws
- 1-in. wire nails
- pin-style shelf supports
- tapered shims
- 1x4 oak lumber
- ¼-in. oak plywood
- 1x3 oak face frames
- 2x4 header and sill plates
- stain & varnish
- wood putty
- sandpaper

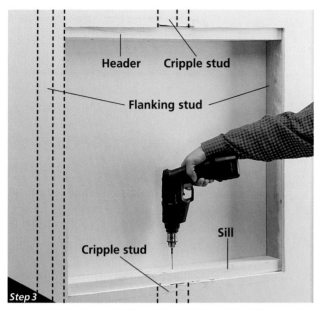

Secure the header and sill to the cripple and flanking studs.

Step 4

A. Measure the height of the opening between the header and the sill and the width between the studs.

B. Cut the 1×4 shelf side pieces 1¾ in. shorter than the measured height of the opening.

C. Cut the 1×4 top and bottom pieces ¼ in. shorter than the measured width of the opening, to allow for adjustments during installation.

D. Drill two rows of holes on the inside face of each side piece, sized to hold pin-style shelf supports, using a portable drill stand and a scrap piece of pegboard as a template.

If you prefer to install metal shelf standards, you can skip this step.

Step 5

A. To assemble the cabinet, glue and clamp the side pieces over the top and bottom pieces.

B. Drill counterbored pilot holes into the butt joints. Secure them with 1½-in. screws.

C. Measure and cut a ¼-in. plywood back panel flush with the outside edges of the cabinet.

D. Attach the back panel with 1-in. wire nails positioned every 4 to 5 in. along the outer edge.

Step 6

A. Place the cabinet in the opening. Shim it until it's level and plumb and its front edges are flush with the surface of the wall.

B. Drill pilot holes. Secure the cabinet to the flanking studs, header and sill with 1½-in. finishing nails driven every 4 to 5 in. and through each of the shims.

C. Trim the shims even with the cabinet, using a utility knife.

Step 7

A. Measure the inside height and width of the cabinet.

B. Cut 1×3 horizontal pieces equal to the width of the cabinet, and vertical pieces 5 in. longer than its height.

C. Glue and clamp the horizontal pieces between the vertical pieces to form butt joints.

D. Reinforce the joints by drilling pilot holes and driving 3-in. finishing nails through the vertical pieces and into the horizontal pieces.

Step 8

A. Position the face frame around the cabinet. Drill pilot holes and attach it with 1½-in. nails driven into the top, bottom and side panels and the framing members.

B. Set the nails; fill the holes with wood putty.

C. Sand the unit. Finish with stain and varnish.

D. Add shelf pegs. Cut 1×4 shelves ⅛ in. shorter than the measurement inside the cabinet. Sand and finish the shelves; install them in the cabinet.

Shim the cabinet until it's level and plumb, and secure it with nails.

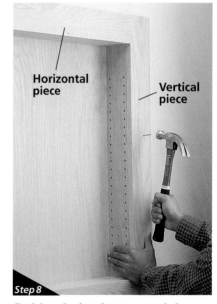

Position the face frame around the cabinet and nail it in place.

KITCHEN WINE RACK

A wine rack in the soffit above your kitchen cabinets is an easy, inexpensive project that can provide elegant storage for a dozen wine bottles. If you collect rare wines, you'll want to store them in a cool room in the cellar. But these recessed nooks are a convenient way to keep everyday wines within easy reach.

The wine rack is easy to construct—it's simply a plywood box framed with decorative molding and installed into the soffit. However, before starting this project, it's important to make sure that there are no heating ducts or hot-water pipes running through the area that could overheat the wine.

Tools

- tape measure
- drywall saw
- jigsaw
- hammer or pry bar
- router with
  ½-in. straight bit
- screwdriver
- nailset
- paintbrush & tools

Materials

- ½-in. birch plywood (½ sheet)
- ¼-in. plywood or hardboard
- 4d (1½-in.) finishing nails
- ¾-in. wire nails
- 1⅛-in. decorative doorstop molding
- ¾-in. flat screen molding
- ¾-in. brads
- wood glue
- wood putty
- 1¾-in. wood screws
- paint

Step 1

A. Cut a small hole in the wall with a drywall saw. Proceed only if you don't see any obstructions in the soffit or any heat sources (such as ducts or pipes) nearby. If you do, patch the hole and choose another spot.

B. Mark and cut a 9×26-in. hole in the soffit with a drywall saw. If the bottom of the framing extends into the opening, create more space by cutting it lengthwise with a jigsaw. Pry out the waste with a hammer or pry bar.

Step 2

A. There will most likely be at least one stud in the hole. Pull the nails that secure it in place.

B. Move that stud to the left edge, screwing it to the top and bottom framing.

C. Move or add a stud on the right edge as well.

Step 3

A. Cut two 9×11-in. pieces of ½-in. plywood for the sides of the rack.

B. Cut three 11×25-in. pieces of ½-in. plywood for the top, bottom and horizontal shelf.

C. Cut ten 4×11-in. pieces of ½-in. plywood for the vertical dividers.

D. Cut one 9×26-in. piece of ¼-in. plywood or hardboard for the back.

Step 4

Using a router with a ½-in. straight bit, cut ⅛-in.-deep × ½-in.-wide grooves in the top, bottom and shelf, spaced 4¼ in. on center.

Step 5

A. Nail the top and bottom pieces between the two sides with finishing nails. Secure the back with wire nails.

B. Slide the horizontal shelf into the plywood box. Secure to the box with finishing nails.

C. Spread glue into the grooves and slide the vertical dividers into them. Let the glue dry.

Step 6

A. Miter the doorstop molding to fit around the perimeter of the rack, allowing it to extend over the outer edge by ⅛ in. Attach it with wood glue and brads.

B. Attach the screen molding to the shelf and the vertical dividers with brads.

C. Set and fill all the nail holes with putty.

D. Slide the rack into the wall opening. Drive two screws into the upper frame and one screw into each side. Paint the wine rack to match the surrounding wall.

If necessary, cut along the bottom of the soffit. Pry out the waste, taking care not to damage the surrounding drywall.

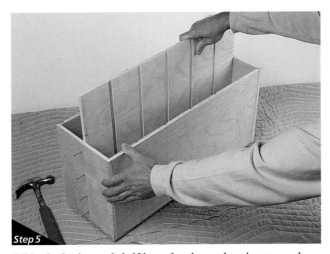

Slide the horizontal shelf into the plywood perimeter and attach it to the sides and back of the box with finishing nails.

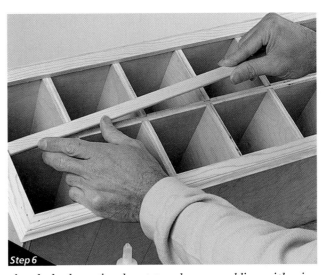

Attach the decorative doorstop and screen molding with wire brads. Set the brads and fill all the holes with wood putty.

STAIRWAY PANTRY

The wall of a basement stairwell is the ideal spot for a trio of recessed cabinets. The 14½-in. bays between standard wall studs are just the right size for these spacious custom-made pantry shelves.

Choose an interior wall with enough room behind it for cabinets of a desirable depth, such as a partition wall that encloses a basement staircase. If the staircase doesn't have a partition wall, you can build a 2×4 stud wall to hold the cabinets.

We built these cabinets out of birch-veneer plywood, using ¾-in. plywood for the sides, tops, bottoms and shelves, and ¼-in. plywood for the backs.

Step 1

A. Cut the rough openings in the wall for the cabinets.

B. Using the 16d nails, attach 2×4 sill plates between the studs, keeping them about 3 in. above the stair stringer. The existing top plate and wall studs will form the top and sides of the openings.

Step 2

A. Carefully measure the height, width and depth of each rough opening to get the starting dimensions for the three cabinet frames.

B. To ensure easy installation, size the cabinets ⅛ in. smaller than the dimensions of the rough openings.

C. Cut the sides, tops and bottoms of the plywood frames to size with a table saw or a circular saw.

D. Glue and screw the pieces together with simple butt joints, using 1⅝-in. wood screws.

E. Cut the back panels to the overall dimensions of each frame. Fasten one side edge of the back to the frame with the wood screws. Check for square, then fasten the remaining edges.

Materials
- 2x4 sill plates
- ¾-in. birch-veneer plywood
- ¼-in. birch-veneer plywood
- ¾ x 1½-in. oak trim
- ⅛ x ¾-in. oak edge banding
- wood glue
- shelf standards (4 per cabinet)
- shelf support clips (4 per shelf)
- 2-in. & 1⅝-in. wood screws
- 16d common nails
- 2d & 4d finishing nails
- sandpaper
- paint or varnish

Tools
- tape measure
- table saw or portable circular saw
- screwdriver
- drill
- hammer
- painting or staining tools

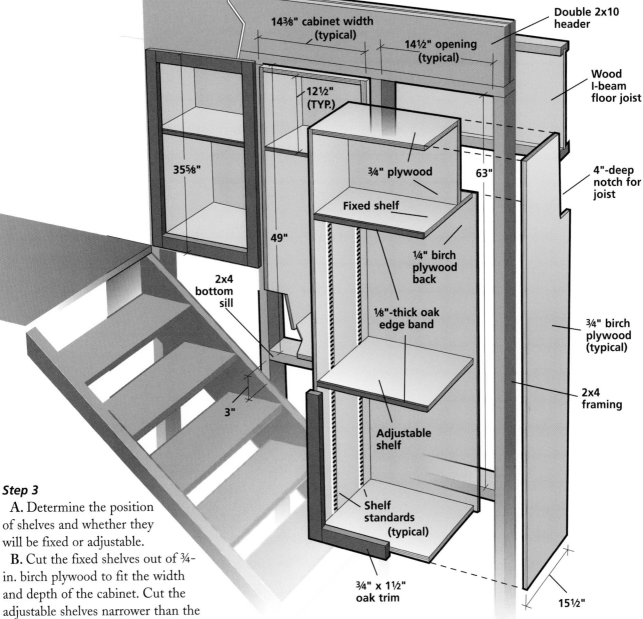

Double 2x10 header

Wood I-beam floor joist

14⅜" cabinet width (typical)

14½" opening (typical)

12½" (TYP.)

¾" plywood

63"

4"-deep notch for joist

35⅝"

Fixed shelf

¼" birch plywood back

49"

⅛"-thick oak edge band

¾" birch plywood (typical)

2x4 bottom sill

Adjustable shelf

2x4 framing

3"

Shelf standards (typical)

¾" x 1½" oak trim

15½"

Step 3

A. Determine the position of shelves and whether they will be fixed or adjustable.

B. Cut the fixed shelves out of ¾-in. birch plywood to fit the width and depth of the cabinet. Cut the adjustable shelves narrower than the fixed shelves to allow for the thickness of the shelf standards, and ⅛ in. shorter to allow for the oak edge banding.

C. Glue and screw the fixed shelves to the cabinet sides and back, using 1⅝-in. screws.

D. Glue the oak edge banding to the front edge of the adjustable shelves.

E. Attach the shelf standards for the adjustable shelves to the side walls of the cabinet, 1½ in. from the front and back of the cabinets.

Step 4

A. Cut ¾ × 1½-in. oak trim to fit around the front edges of the cabinets. Center the trim on the front edges of the cabinets to create a ⅜-in. overhanging lip on both sides of the cabinet panels.

B. Glue and nail the trim to the cabinets and the front edges of the fixed shelves, using 4d nails.

C. Place the cabinets in the openings and shim until level.

D. Secure the cabinets with twelve

2-in. wood screws driven through the sides of the cabinet and into the wall studs.

Step 5

A. Smooth all the surfaces and edges of the pantry with sandpaper.

B. Apply two coats of polyurethane varnish or paint to protect the pantry from wear and dirt accumulation.

WALL-TO-WALL BOOKCASES

It can be surprisingly easy and affordable to create an impressive wall-to-wall bookcase such as this one. The trick is to assemble it from the wall cabinets made by kitchen cabinet companies or the knock-down cabinets that are sold in furniture stores.

Step 1

A. Make a drawing of the existing wall space, including all the dimensions. Take it to a showroom, home center or lumberyard.

B. Show the salesperson your drawing and describe your built-in project. Inspect the cabinets on dis-

play. Ask to see planning guides as well as manufacturers' catalogs.

C. Choose a cabinet style and select specific sizes and features from the planning guide.

Step 2

A. Position the base cabinets; use shims to level them.

B. Screw the base cabinets together through the face-frame stiles, using 2½-in. screws placed 4 in. from the top and the bottom.

C. Secure the base assembly to the wall studs with 3-in. screws. Don't overtighten them, or the doors and drawers won't operate properly.

Step 3

A. Using 2½-in. screws, attach the upper cabinets together as you did the base cabinets.

B. Place the upper cabinets onto the base cabinets as a single unit. (If you prefer, you can also install them individually and then fasten them together.)

C. Attach the upper cabinets to the wall, using 3-in. screws.

Step 4

Trim the bookcase with baseboard and crown molding that matches the trim used in the rest of the room as closely as possible.

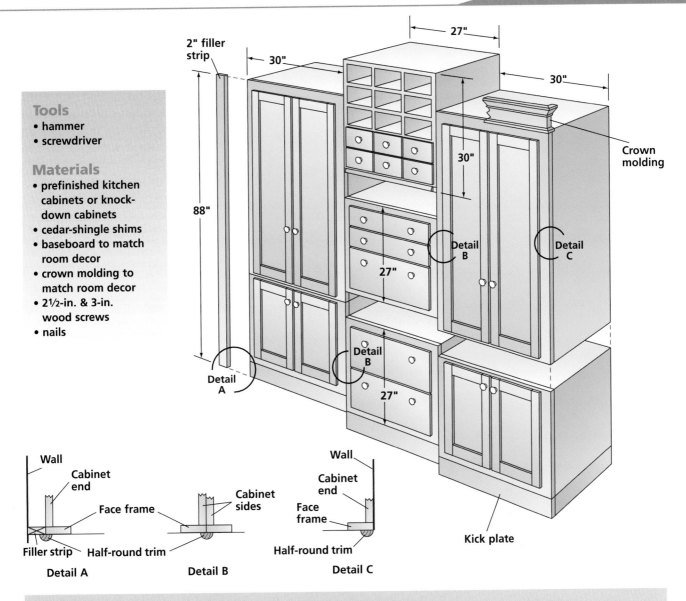

Tools
- hammer
- screwdriver

Materials
- prefinished kitchen cabinets or knock-down cabinets
- cedar-shingle shims
- baseboard to match room decor
- crown molding to match room decor
- 2½-in. & 3-in. wood screws
- nails

2" filler strip

30"

27"

30"

88"

30"

27"

Crown molding

Detail B

Detail C

Detail B

27"

Detail A

Wall

Cabinet end

Face frame

Filler strip

Half-round trim

Detail A

Cabinet sides

Half-round trim

Detail B

Wall

Cabinet end

Face frame

Half-round trim

Detail C

Kick plate

CHOOSING CABINETS

To determine the quality of the cabinets you're considering for your built-in projects, ask these questions:
- How are the cabinets constructed? What material are the carcasses made from?
- Are the drawer sides made of solid wood or plywood? Check for sturdy metal drawer slides and strong dovetail or rabbet joints.
- Do the doors have self-closing hinges that are easy to adjust?
- Are the doorknobs, drawer pulls and shelf hardware included?
- Is the finish water- and alcohol-resistant? (Important for areas where food or drink will be served.)

- Are matching filler strips, moldings and trim pieces available?
- Will someone from the showroom come to my house to take exact measurements? (If not, you'll be responsible if something doesn't fit.)
- Once an order is placed, how long will it take for the cabinets to arrive?
- Is there a delivery charge to bring the cabinets to the house?
- Is installation available?
- What will the cabinets cost? (While you won't get an exact figure until you place the order, you should be able to get a rough idea of the cost.)

ENTERTAINMENT CENTER

This handsome cherry entertainment center is built entirely from stock kitchen cabinets. The upper half of the center cabinet houses the television and the VCR; its base cabinet has three roll-out shelves for videos and supplies.

Good-looking home entertainment centers like this one are usually expensive to buy and difficult to build from scratch. However, stock kitchen cabinets offer a timesaving shortcut for the do-it-yourselfer. Once we had all the materials, it took just two days to assemble the cabinets.

This unit is composed of five stock cabinets. The center television unit is a 36-in.-wide × 84-in.-tall utility cabinet, turned upside down. Flanking it on either side is a standard 18-in.-wide × 30-in.-tall wall cabinet, topped by a 48-in.-tall bookcase.

Tools
- screwdriver
- drill
- portable circular saw
- hammer
- clamps

Materials
- 36-in.-wide x 84-in.-tall utility cabinet
- 18-in.-wide x 30-in.-tall wall cabinets (2)
- 48-in.-tall bookcases (2)
- matching plywood skins
- matching crown molding
- matching 1x4
- matching cove molding
- $3/4$-in. plywood or 2x4s (base)
- $3/4$-in. plywood (TV shelf panel)
- roll-out shelves & mounting hardware
- $3/4$-in. x 1-in. wood strips
- contact cement
- 2d & 4d finishing nails
- $2^{1/2}$-in. wood screws

When building with stock kitchen cabinets, the biggest challenge is making the finished project look like custom furniture rather than a bunch of stacked-up boxes. The secret is in the accents—the baseboard, molding, shelves, fluted filler strips, prefinished skins and glass-paned doors—that are offered by cabinet manufacturers specifically for this purpose.

Building with stock units does require you to sacrifice some design features. For example, most stock cabinets don't come with slide-back doors. However, our television cabinet has hinges that open to 170 degrees—more than enough for a clear view of the set.

Also, most kitchen cabinets aren't finished on the inside. Although you might not mind staining them yourself, we wanted an exact match throughout the unit, so we bought prefinished plywood "skins" and glued them to the inner surfaces of the cabinets. This is optional, but it makes the unit as attractive with the doors open as it is when they're closed.

Before you buy your cabinets, carefully measure each piece of equipment you plan to put inside them, including any wires, jacks or picture tubes that project from the back, and any knobs that stick out in front. Figure out where you'll need to drill holes in the cabinet backs and shelves to run the electrical wiring. Also be sure to allow enough space around electrical components to avoid overheating.

Here are the steps we followed to assemble this entertainment center; they will remain essentially the same for any stock cabinets you choose.

Step 1

Remove the baseboard molding from the wall where the entertainment center will be placed.

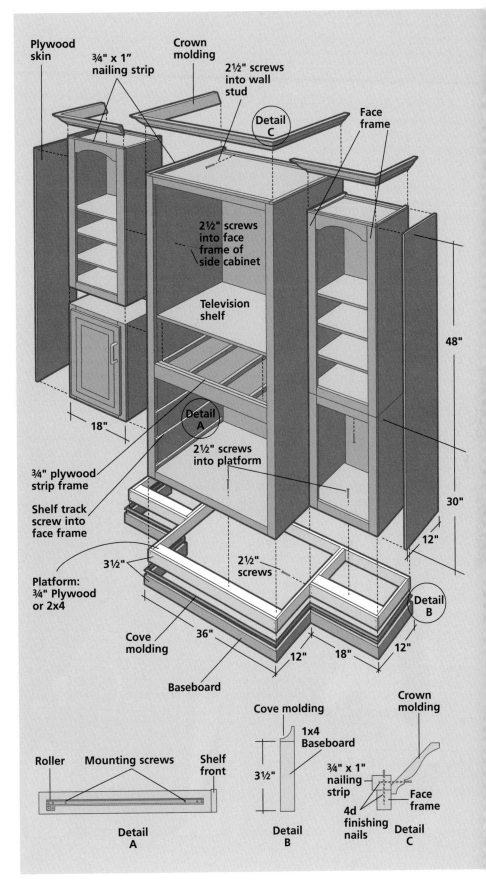

Plywood skin

¾" x 1" nailing strip

Crown molding

2½" screws into wall stud

Detail C

Face frame

2½" screws into face frame of side cabinet

Television shelf

48"

18"

¾" plywood strip frame

Shelf track screw into face frame

Detail A

2½" screws into platform

30"

12"

Platform: ¾" Plywood or 2x4

3½"

2½" screws

Detail B

Cove molding

36"

12"

18"

12"

Baseboard

Roller   Mounting screws   Shelf front

Detail A

Cove molding

3½"

1x4 Baseboard

Detail B

Crown molding

¾" x 1" nailing strip

4d finishing nails

Face frame

Detail C

Step 2

Build a 3½-in.-high base platform for the cabinets, as shown in the photo. (The platform raises the cabinets off the floor and will be concealed by baseboard molding.)

Make the platform out of ¾-in. plywood or 2×4s set on edge, to the exact dimensions of the cabinets. If you make it out of plywood, you can add a front backing strip to provide extra support, as shown. Fasten the pieces together with 2½-in. screws.

Step 3

A. Using a portable circular saw, carefully cut off the toekick on the bottom of the large utility cabinet.

B. Flip the cabinet upside down so that the larger compartment is on top. Set the cabinet on the center of the platform.

Step 4

Build up the height of the television shelf so its surface is flush with the face frame. (This will make it easier to slide in the television and access the control buttons.)

A. Cut four or five narrow plywood strips. To determine their width, measure the height of the face frame from the shelf bottom, and subtract the width of the plywood panel (and the plywood skin, if you're using one).

B. Lay the strips across the shelf, equally spaced. Secure with glue and toenailed 2d finishing nails.

C. Cut a ¾-in. plywood panel to fit over the strips. Secure it in place with 4d finishing nails. (Always drill pilot holes before screwing or nailing into the stock cabinets.)

Step 5

A. Clamp one of the bookcase units to one of the wall cabinet units. Drive a pair of 2½-in. screws through the cabinet frame and into the bookcase frame.

B. Lay the assembled unit on its side on a blanket or pad.

C. Cut a plywood skin to span the exposed side of both cabinets to conceal the joint between them. Glue it down with contact cement.

D. Repeat steps 5A to 5D for the other bookcase.

Step 6

A. Place the two assembled bookcase units onto the platform. Attach them to the middle television cabinet, drilling pilot holes first. Drive the screws through the side of the cabinet and into the face frame of the bookcase.

B. Drive a 2½-in. screw through the bottom of each of the base cabinets and into the platform below.

C. Drive a screw through the upper rear panel of each cabinet and into a wall stud.

Step 7

A. Cut the prefinished plywood skins for the interior surfaces of the television compartment.

B. Glue the plywood skins in place with contact cement, starting with the one that covers the inside top of the cabinet.

C. Glue the plywood skin over the raised bottom shelf.

Since this surface may not be visible (depending on the size of your television), you may prefer to stain the shelf instead.

D. Install the plywood skin on the back of the cabinet.

E. Install the plywood skin on the left- and right-side panels.

Build a 3½-in.-high platform base to support the cabinets.

Use a circular saw to cut the toekick off the bottom of the large utility cabinet.

Use wood strips and plywood to raise the TV shelf even with the face frame.

Step 5

Step 6

Step 7

Fasten a wall cabinet to a bookcase with two screws into the face frames.

Secure the cabinets by screwing through the upper panel and into wall studs.

Line the interior of the TV cabinet with prefinished plywood skins.

Step 8

A. Screw the metal tracks that support the roll-out shelves into the bottom of the television cabinet.

B. Fasten the front end of each track to the edge of the cabinet face frame.

Step 9

Install the specialty hardware and decorative trim, as follows:

A. Hide the platform below the cabinets with a matching baseboard secured with 4d finishing nails. We used a solid 1×4 topped with a cove molding secured with 2d nails.

B. Nail ¾ × 1-in. wood strips along the tops of the cabinets, flush with the outside edge, to provide fastening support for the crown molding.

C. Miter-cut the matching crown

molding to size.

D. Drill pilot holes and nail the crown molding to the strips, using 4d finishing nails.

Step 10

A. Cut the old baseboard to fit the remaining wall alongside the new wall unit.

B. Install your TV and entertainment equipment.

Step 8

Step 9

Step 10

Attach the metal tracks for the roll-out shelves to the edge of the face frame.

Conceal the platform with a 1×4 topped with a cove molding.

Miter-cut the crown molding, prebore pilot holes and nail it into place.

FLOOR-TO-CEILING SHELVES

A wall of floor-to-ceiling shelves allows you to transform an ordinary room into an inviting den or library. Built-in shelves are also sturdier and make better use of space than a freestanding bookcase. For the best results, select a wood finish and trim that matches the room's existing wall moldings.

A built-in bookcase isn't literally "built into" the wall, but installed against it. Since only the front, and perhaps one side, of the bookcase is exposed, it appears to be recessed into the wall. For this project, we used finish-grade oak plywood and a solid oak face frame that gives the shelves the look of an expensive solid oak shelving unit, at a fraction of the cost.

If you're installing floor-to-ceiling shelves in a corner, as shown here, you'll need to add ½-in. plywood spacers to the support studs that adjoin the wall. The spacers will ensure that you can install face frame stiles of equal width on both sides of the unit.

This is a challenging project that requires good carpentry skills and may take a few weekends to complete—but the final outcome will be well worth the effort.

Step 1

A. Mark the location of two parallel 2×4 top plates on the ceiling, using a framing square as a guide. Mark the front edge of the outer top plate 13 in. from the back wall and the other top plate flush against the wall.

B. Mark the location of the ceiling joists. If necessary, install blocking between them to create a surface on which to anchor the top plates.

C. Measure and cut the top plates from 2×4 lumber.

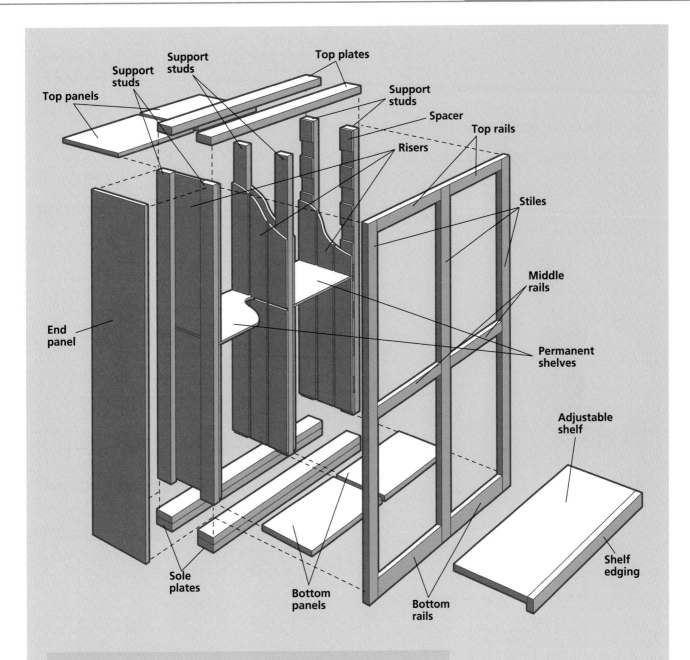

Top plates

Support studs

Support studs

Top panels

Support studs

Spacer

Top rails

Risers

Stiles

End panel

Middle rails

Permanent shelves

Adjustable shelf

Sole plates

Bottom panels

Bottom rails

Shelf edging

Tools
- ruler or tape measure
- framing square
- screwdriver
- hammer
- drill with ¾-in. straight bit
- plumb bob
- level
- router
- sander
- circular saw
- paintbrush

Materials
- 2x4 lumber (top & bottom plates, support studs)
- ½-in. plywood
- ¾-in. plywood
- 1x3 lumber (stiles & top rails)
- 1x4 bottom rails
- metal shelf standards & clips
- wood glue
- shims
- 1¾-in., 2-in. & 3-in. screws
- 4d (1½-in.) finishing nails
- shelf-edge molding
- paint or stain

D. Place each plate in position. Level them, shimming if necessary. Attach the plates to the ceiling with 3-in. screws driven into the joists or blocking.

Step 1

Position the top plates and level them. Attach them with screws driven into the ceiling joists or blocking.

Step 2

A. Cut four bottom plates from 2×4 lumber. Screw them together to form two double-high bottom plates.

B. Align the bottom plates with the top plates, using a plumb bob suspended from the outside corners of the top plates. Shim the bottom plates to level them.

C. Anchor the plates with 3-in. screws toescrewed into the floor.

Step 3

A. Cut the six support studs from 2×4 lumber. Install four of them at the corners of the unit with 3-in. screws toescrewed through the studs and into the plates.

B. Install the center support studs midway between the end support studs. Toescrew them to the bottom plate first with 3-in. screws. Use a level to make sure that the studs are plumb, then attach them to the top plate.

Step 4

A. Where the shelves fit into a corner, use 2-in. screws to attach ½-in. plywood spacers on the inside faces of the support studs, spaced every 4 in. Don't extend the spacers past the front edge of the studs.

B. If the side of the unit will be exposed, cut a ½-in. plywood end panel to the floor-to-ceiling height.

C. Attach the panel to the support studs with the front edges flush, driving 1¾-in. screws through the support studs into the end panel.

D. Measure and cut ½-in. plywood panels to fit between the support studs on the top and bottom of the unit. Attach them to the top and bottom plates with 1½-in. (4d) finishing nails.

Step 3

Install the center support studs midway between the end support studs.

Step 4

Attach an end panel to the support studs on the exposed side of the unit.

Step 5

Measure, cut and install the upper risers above the permanent shelves.

Step 5

A. Measure and cut the lower risers from ½-in. plywood. Cut grooves in them to hold the metal shelf standards.

B. Install the lower risers on each side of the 2×4 support studs so the front edges are flush with the edges of the studs. Secure the risers to the support studs with 1½-in. (4d) finishing nails. On the riser that adjoins the wall, drive the nails through the spacers.

C. Measure and cut the permanent shelves from ¾-in. plywood to fit between the support studs, just above the lower risers.

D. Set the shelves on the risers and attach them with 1½-in. (4d) finishing nails driven down into the risers.

E. Measure and cut the upper risers to fit between the permanent shelves and the top panels. Cut grooves in the risers to hold the metal shelf standards. Nail the risers to the support studs.

Step 6

A. Measure and cut 1×3 stiles to fit from the floor to the ceiling along the front edges of the exposed support studs.

B. Drill pilot holes and attach the stiles to the support studs so they're flush with the risers, using glue and finishing nails driven at 8-in. intervals into the studs and risers.

C. Measure and cut 1×3 top rails to fit between the stiles. Drill pilot holes and attach the rails to the top plate and top panels with glue and finishing nails.

D. Measure and cut 1×4 bottom rails to fit between the stiles. Drill pilot holes and attach the rails to the bottom plates and bottom panels, as above. The top edge of the rails should be flush with the top surface of the plywood panels.

Step 7

A. Fill all the nail holes. Sand and finish all the wood surfaces.

B. Measure, cut and install metal shelf standards in the riser grooves, using the nails or screws that come with the standards.

C. Measure and cut the adjustable shelves ⅛ in. shorter than the distance between the metal shelf standards.

D. Cut the shelf-edge molding; attach it to the shelves with glue and finishing nails.

E. Sand and finish the shelves.

Step 8

A. Insert shelf clips into the metal shelf standards.

B. Install the adjustable shelves.

C. Cover any gaps between the floor-to-ceiling shelving unit and the walls and floor with a molding that's been finished to match the shelving.

Attach the stiles and rails to the front edge of the unit.

Cover gaps at the walls and floor with matching molding.

LIGHTING A WALL UNIT

Tools
- router
- drill with hole saw or Forstner bit

Materials
- plastic wire tracks
- plastic wire organizers
- 12V transformer
- vent screens
- outlet strips
- grommet plates

Adding electrical accessories to a wall unit can make it both more attractive and more useful. For example, low-voltage halogen lights can turn an ordinary bookcase into an elegant display case; these fixtures use very little electricity and can be left on permanently. And adding an electrical outlet strip to an entertainment center allows you to connect electronic equipment without using cumbersome extension cords.

When adding lights or other electrical accessories to a wall unit, try to keep the wires hidden from view. Inexpensive wire organizers and wire tracks inside the built-in can help hide the cords and keep them neat.

If the unit contains incandescent lights or electronic equipment, such as a television, computer or stereo, it's a good idea to install vent screens in the shelves or walls to dissipate the heat they generate.

To provide a convenient place to plug in electronic components or light fixtures, you can attach an outlet strip inside the unit. Some models have a remote on-off switch that will control up to four receptacles, a telephone jack or a cable TV outlet. For computer equipment, use a strip that has power-surge protection.

Vent screens dissipate the heat generated by electrical gear.

Installing Halogen Lights

Step 1

Cut holes in the top panel of the wall unit to accommodate the low-voltage light fixtures.

Cut small grooves into the shelves and risers for the wires.

Step 2

Install the low-voltage light fixtures, running the wires through the grooves.

Cover the wires with plastic wire tracks in the grooves. Leave several inches of space around the lights to prevent heat accumulation.

Step 3

Install a 12V transformer to convert the 120V current from an ordinary wall receptacle to low-voltage power for the lights.

Hiding wires

Here are some ideas that can help hide the electrical wires that provide light and power to your wall unit or cabinet:

• Cut a plastic wire organizer to the desired length and tack it inside the cabinet to keep electrical cords and cables neatly tucked away out of sight (photo, right).

• Drill a hole to run cords and cables through the side of the unit or cabinet. To reduce the chance of splintering, use a hole saw or a Forstner bit.

• Install grommet plates over the holes, slipping the groove in the grommet around the wires (photo, below).

• Grommets are available in a variety of materials and finishes. For a coordinated look, select hardwood grommets, which can be stained to match the color of your wall unit.

Wire organizers hide cords and cables.

MINIATURE LIGHT SYSTEMS

Miniature light systems are available in both low and regular voltage, and fall into four main categories: mini-tracks, strips, pucks and fluorescents. Low-voltage systems require a transformer but offer greater energy efficiency and smaller lights.

Mini-tracks. Miniature versions of track lighting, the tracks can be cut to length and run almost anywhere with connectors that can turn corners. Bulbs can be placed anywhere along the track.

Strip lighting. These bulbs are set in a fixed pattern and usually left exposed. However, this is a good option inside cabinets, and less costly than mini-tracks.

Puck lights. Low-voltage halogen puck lights are good for display-case or undercabinet lighting. You can adjust the direction of the light, and some can be recessed within a shelf.

Fluorescent fixtures. These fixtures, often used under cabinets to light a countertop, have narrow tubes and a plastic cover to diffuse the light.

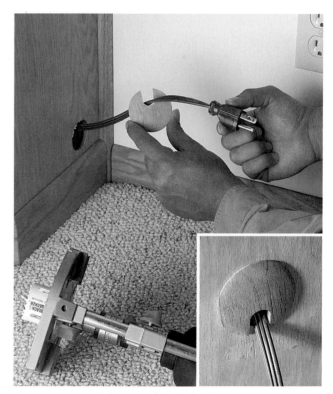

Grommet plates help conceal the holes for cords and cables.

GLIDE-OUT SHELVES

Adding full-extension glide-out shelves to a base cabinet helps make more efficient use of hard-to-reach storage space by providing easier access to items tucked in the back.

Glide-out and roll-out shelf extensions are most common in kitchen cabinets, but they have many other uses, as well. For example, roll-out shelves are also used in the entertainment center (pages 118-121).

Step 1

A. Determine the width of the glide-out shelves by measuring the inside of the cabinet and subtracting 3½ in. This allows space for two standards and brackets (1¼ in. each) and two slides (½ in. each).

B. Cut two 1×4s to that measurement for each shelf. These will be the front and back pieces. Use a jigsaw to cut out the top edge of the front pieces to make a drawer pull.

C. Cut two 21¼ in.-long pieces for the sides of each shelf.

D. Cut the bottom from ½-in. birch plywood.

Step 2

A. Rout a ⅜-in.-deep × ½-in.-wide groove into each 1×4, ½ in. up

Tools	Materials
• tape measure	• 8-ft. 1x4 poplar (2)
• level	• ½-in. birch plywood (½ sheet)
• jigsaw	• full-extension drawer slides (2 per shelf)
• circular saw	• shelf standards (2 sets)
• router with ½-in. straight bit	• brackets (4 per shelf)
	• wood glue
• hammer	• 4d (1½-in.) finishing nails
• finishing sander	• 120-grit sandpaper
• screwdriver	• 180-grit sandpaper
	• sanding sealer

Step 2

Rout grooves and rabbets in the 1×4s.

from the bottom edge.

B. Cut a ⅜-in.-deep × ¾-in.-wide rabbet across the inside face of each end of the shelf front and back.

C. Spread glue onto the shelf front rabbets and attach the shelf sides, using three 4d finishing nails.

D. Spread a bead of glue along the groove in the shelf front; slide the bottom into place. Glue and nail on the shelf back. Clamp the pieces square and let the glue dry.

E. Smooth all surfaces with a finishing sander and 120-grit sandpaper. Wipe off all dust and coat the shelf with sanding sealer. Let dry for one hour.

F. Lightly hand-sand the shelf with 180-grit sandpaper. Apply a second coat of sealer.

Apply glue to the rabbet joint and nail the front of the shelf to the sides.

Step 3

A. Position the front standards 2½ in. from the inside edge of the face frame. On a frameless cabinet, measure from the front edge of the cabinet.

B. Use a level to make sure the standards are perfectly vertical, then secure them with screws.

C. Install the rear standards 17¹/₁₆ in. from the first set, measuring from center to center.

D. Bolt two metal shelf standard brackets to each drawer slide, making sure they're 17¹/₁₆ in. on center.

Step 4

A. Mount the drawer slides to the cabinet by snapping the metal clips into the slots in the standards.

B. Detach the sliding rail from each slide by pressing down on the release lever.

C. Screw a sliding rail to each side of the shelves, ½ in. up from the bottom edge.

D. Install each shelf by aligning its sliding rails with the slides inside the cabinet and pushing it all the way in. The rails will automatically lock into place.

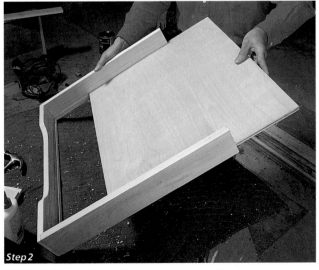

Slide the bottom into the grooves; glue and nail on the back.

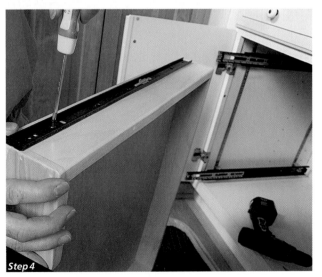

Attach a sliding rail to each side of the shelves.

ADDING SHELVING & STORAGE

Improving Your Yard

Turn your yard and
deck into an elegant,
relaxing outdoor
retreat, in just a
few weekends.

Redwood arbor photo courtesy of California Redwood Association

*I*mproving Your Yard

QUICK REFERENCE		
YARD	*Stepping–Stone Path*	*page 134*
	Outdoor Lighting	*page 136*
	Garden Pond	*page 138*
DECK RAILINGS	*Eastern Influence*	*page 142*
	Cedar Louvers	*page 143*
DECK ADD-ONS	*Tiered Planters*	*page 144*
	Privacy Screen	*page 145*
	Cozy Corner	*page 146*
FENCES	*Crossrail Classic*	*page 148*
	Redwood Slats	*page 149*
GATES & ARBORS	*Patio Arbor*	*page 150*
	Cedar Settee	*page 154*

If your "great outdoors" consists of an unadorned yard or a basic deck, don't despair. Consider this simply your blank canvas for creating a beautiful, welcoming outdoor living area. In this chapter, you'll find many ideas that you can use to transform your yard into a private retreat in a weekend or two.

Most of the projects in this section require solid carpentry skills and experience, especially the outdoor structures, so don't attempt one of these as your first woodworking project.

Before starting one of these projects, read over the instructions to make sure you understand all the tools, skills and techniques involved. If you'd like to try a yard addition that doesn't fall within your skill level, try an easier one first to build your skills, or arrange to get expert help from a friend or neighbor.

Yard Improvements

Even one weekend yard improvement can make a big difference in the beauty and value of your home. For example, a stepping-stone path is an easy way to pave a well-traveled passage or to add an interesting new element to your landscape. One of the most useful yard improvements is outdoor lighting. In just a few hours, you can install a light system that will improve the safety and security of your property and highlight the best features of your yard.

A water garden can add a tranquil touch to any yard, whether it's a simple tub of aquatic plants or a lavish in-ground goldfish pond. As you'll see here, creating a water garden is surprisingly easy—two people can install a basic pond in a weekend.

Deck Railings & Add-Ons

Railings, benches, planters, screens—additions such as these can transform a nondescript deck into an inviting place to relax, entertain and enjoy the outdoors. Remodeling an old deck is an economical, creative alternative to replacing it, and most of these deck additions can be completed in one or two weekends.

Before beginning any deck project, inspect your present structure to make sure it's free of rot and defects. Check the understructure framing, posts, joists, beams and ledger, and replace any failing parts.

Fences, Gates & Arbors

If you have good carpentry skills and are looking for an impressive outdoor project, a fence, gate or shade arbor is a good choice. These outdoor structures are functional, appealing ways to provide a peaceful rest area, a backdrop for vines or flowers or an impressive boundary or entry.

These projects require a complete set of portable power tools, so be prepared. Also, since these are permanent structures, they're regulated by local zoning and building codes.

Before breaking ground, you'll need to submit your plans to your local building department and get a permit.

STEPPING-STONE PATH

Tools
- spade
- garden rake

Materials
- sand or compactible gravel
- stepping-stones

Whether you'd like to pave a frequently traveled route or simply introduce a sense of movement to your landscape, a stepping-stone path can be an ideal and inexpensive solution. A thoughtfully arranged stepping-stone path almost begs to be walked upon, and its open design will complement, rather than overpower, the rest of your landscape.

When planning a stepping-stone path, bear in mind that a design with gentle curves is usually more attractive than a straight one. Also, consider the distance between the stones; set the stones to accommodate a normal stride, so you'll be able to step effortlessly from one stone to the next.

Step 1

Step 3

Step 4

Arrange the stepping-stones on top of the grass, then test the layout by walking over them in a normal stride.

Dig out the outlined areas 2 in. deeper than the height of the stones. Spread a 2-in. layer of sand in each hole.

Reposition the stones in the holes. Add or remove sand as needed until they're stable and flush with the ground.

There are many materials that are suitable for a stepping-stone path, from natural stone to wood to concrete. To ensure that your path will blend in with the rest of your landscape, try to repeat a material that's used in other parts of your yard.

A local stone is usually a good choice, as it's likely to be inexpensive and to appear natural and familiar. Many stone yards sell 1- to 2½-in.-thick sedimentary rock "steppers," which are ideal for stepping-stone paths. You can also use cut stone, wood rounds, or precast concrete pavers.

Also keep safety in mind. Select steppers that are wide enough to stand on comfortably, have a flat, even surface and have enough texture so that they don't become slick or slippery when wet.

It's important to prepare the sand or gravel base carefully—without a proper base, stepping-stones can become unstable or settle unevenly. Also, check the path after the ground thaws each spring, and adjust the height of the stones if they've been raised or lowered by the freeze-thaw cycle.

Step 1

A. Arrange the stepping-stones on the ground along your planned pathway.

B. Walk the full course of the path, using a natural, easy stride.

C. Adjust the spacing of the steppers until you can step smoothly and easily from stone to stone. Make any final adjustments needed to get a pleasing design.

Step 2

A. If you're installing the path over grass or another living ground cover, leave the stones in place for three to five days. The plants beneath the stones will die, leaving a perfect outline of the stones on the ground.

B. If you're installing the path over gravel, wood chips or another non-living material, scratch an outline around each stone.

Step 3

A. Using a spade, cut around each outline and dig down 2 in. deeper than the thickness of the stones.

B. Add a 2-in. layer of sand or compactible gravel to the holes; smooth it level with a garden rake.

Step 4

A. Place the stones in the partially filled holes. Rock each stone back and forth several times to make sure it settles securely into the base.

B. Check to make sure the stepping stones are stable and flush with the ground. To readjust the stones, add or remove sand or gravel from the base.

Step 5

If you wish, you can plant a low-lying, spreading ground cover between the stones. Plants that work well with stepping-stone paths include thyme, *Lobelia, Sedum,* rock cress, miniature *Dianthus,* Scotch and Irish moss, blue star creeper and Indian mock strawberry.

Low-voltage lighting fixtures operate on far less electricity than a standard electrical circuit, thanks to a transformer that steps down the power. Because of this, these lights are safe to use outside—they won't give you anything but a very mild, harmless shock.

Outdoor lighting offers a yard many benefits, including greater safety, beauty and convenience. However, a few well-placed lights work best, so don't just install the lights randomly. Adding more lights than you need just tends to create an annoying glare.

A little planning can ensure that your outdoor lighting will be both attractive and useful. For example, gather some friends one evening and ask them to hold flashlights the way you're thinking of installing the light fixtures. Check the view from many angles (including inside the house) and adjust the layout until you get the effect you want.

LIGHT YOUR WAY

Here are some tips for getting the best effect when lighting a walkway:
• Avoid the "runway" look that's created by placing lights opposite each other. If you want lights on both sides of a walkway, stagger them.
• When lighting a curve, place the lights on the inside. You'll use fewer fixtures and the effect will be more dramatic.
• The fixtures along a walkway should direct light down to the ground, not up in the air.
• As in other parts of the yard, don't use more lighting fixtures than you need.

Tools	Materials
• screwdriver	• low-voltage lighting kit
• wire cutters	• transformer
• spade	• outdoor lighting cable
	• light fixtures
	• low-voltage bulbs
	• controls

Step 1

A. Choose the locations in the yard for the low-voltage lights.

B. Consider first the areas you need to light for safety, such as stairs, walkways and driveways.

C. Identify other areas to accent or highlight, such as interesting plant groupings, trees or statues.

Step 2

A. Plug the transformer into an outdoor outlet equipped with a ground-fault circuit-interrupter (GFCI).

B. Make sure the outlet is protected by a cover—a weatherproof hinged box that fits over it to keep out moisture.

C. Attach the transformer to a wall or post near the outlet to avoid having to extend the cord.

Step 3

A. Connect the low-voltage cable to the transformer.

B. Run the cable to the fixture locations. Follow the manufacturer's instructions, which typically specify either burying the cable in a 4-in.- deep trench or covering it with mulch. Low-voltage cable does not require conduit.

C. If the cable must cross an open expanse of lawn, you need to bury it. Decide exactly where the fixtures will be placed before digging the trench.

Step 4

A. Connect the fixtures to the cable, following the manufacturer's instructions. Most simply snap directly into the cable.

B. Secure the fixtures according to the instructions. Most fixtures are mounted on bayonet stakes.

Step 5

Dig a shallow hole and set the stake in the ground. Backfill with dirt and small stones. Don't force the fixtures or hammer them into place.

Step 6

After dark, test the system and move the fixtures as needed. Since low-voltage cable seals itself, it's easy to reposition the fixtures.

LIGHTING EFFECTS

Spotlighting. Aim a floodlight at a plant or other yard feature to turn it into a focal point.

Crosslighting. Install two or more fixtures so their beams cross at the object being highlighted. This creates depth and a three-dimensional look.

Backlighting. Place a light behind a feature to make it stand out from its surroundings. This is especially effective when the silhouette falls on a vertical surface, such as a wall.

Uplighting. Install well lights or other short fixtures that cast light upward through the branches of a tree or bush or highlight a statue.

Downlighting (moonlighting). Attach fixtures high in a tree so they cast their light downward through the branches.

Run cable to the fixtures and bury it or cover it with mulch, depending on the manufacturer's instructions.

Connect the fixtures according to the manufacturer's instructions; most simply snap into place.

Turn on the lights and survey the system from several points of view. Make adjustments to get the effect you want.

GARDEN POND

Tools
- rope or garden hose
- digging tools
- straight 2x4
- level
- scissors

Materials
- flexible rubber or PVC pond liner (safe for plants and fish)
- sand
- old carpet or nonfoam underlayment
- bricks or flagstones
- mortar
- water conditioner

Whether it's a simple tub on a patio or a luxuriant pool with plants, fountains and fish, a water garden can enhance any yard. Here we show you how to install a 5×10-ft. pond in a weekend. This pond is large enough for goldfish and aquatic plants, so it doesn't require any pumps or filters to keep it clean. However, you can add a pump to provide water movement.

It's a good idea to make the pond as large as possible, considering your landscape and your budget—the finished pond may look smaller than you expect, and a larger one can be easier to maintain. Choose a level and sunny spot.

Step 1

Determine the size and shape of the pond. A compact shape with gentle, natural curves usually looks and functions best.

Step 2

A. Select a flexible rubber or PVC pond liner that's guaranteed safe for plants and fish.

B. To calculate the size of a flexible liner, first double the depth of the pond. Then add that figure plus 1 ft. to the length and width of the pond. For example, a 5×10-ft., 24-in.-deep pond requires a 10×15-ft. liner.

Step 3

A. Outline the shape of the pond with a rope or garden hose.

B. Dig out the desired shape and depth. The pond must be at least 24 in. deep to keep the water temperature stable for plants and fish.

C. Slope the pond sides gently outward to keep mud and stones from sliding into the pond.

D. Check that the rim is level all around. Lay a straight 2×4 across the excavation at various points and check it with a level.

E. If the pond will have a pump, dig a 12-in.-dia. depression in the bottom, 1 to 2 in. deep.

Step 4

A. Smooth the surface of the excavation and clear away any excess soil and debris.

B. Place a 1- to 2-in. layer of sand on the bottom of the hole to protect the liner from punctures. (For a 5×10-ft. pond this will require 7 to 8 cu. ft. of sand.)

C. Line the edges of the pond with old carpet or a nonfoam underlayment.

Start by outlining the size and shape of the pond with a garden hose.

Step 5

A. Open the liner and allow it to soften in the sun. Don't put it on the lawn—heat buildup under the liner can kill grass in 10 minutes.

B. Spread the liner in the hole, making sure it overlaps all the edges evenly.

C. Smooth out any big wrinkles. Tuck and fold the liner to fit curves and angles.

D. Place a few bricks or stones around the perimeter to hold the liner in place. Don't use too many, or the liner will stretch rather than settle as it's filled with water.

After setting the liner in place and smoothing it, anchor the overhang with stones.

Step 6

A. Slowly fill the pond with water to within 1 in. of the rim.

B. Using scissors, trim off the excess liner, leaving a 12-in. overhang that will go beneath the edging.

C. Lay flagstones or bricks on the overhang along the perimeter of the pond. Lay one of the stones ½ in. lower than the rest to serve as an overflow point for excess water.

For added stability, you can place the stones or bricks in a shallow layer of mortar. Since the mortar will raise the pH of the water, drain the pool afterward and refill it with fresh water.

D. If the pond will be stocked with fish, add a water conditioner to remove any heavy metals and chlorine from the water. If your water contains chloramine, you'll need a special formulation.

Step 6

Fill the pond with water. Then add the water plants. Wait at least a week before adding the goldfish and the water snails.

CREATING A MINIATURE WATER GARDEN

If a full-scale garden pond isn't practical in your yard, you can use small accent pools instead.

Birdbaths, barrel planters and vinyl tubs are all easy to convert into water gardens.

Barrel planters

Cypress, cedar and redwood barrels made with tongue-and-groove construction are self-sealing. All you have to do is fill them with water until the wood swells, which creates a watertight seal. This usually takes about 24 hours.

Vintage whiskey barrels

Although vintage whiskey barrels are also self-sealing, you need to scrub and rinse the interior well to remove any acids or alcohol before you add water or plants.

Other barrels

You can make other barrels watertight either by lining them

with heavy-duty plastic sheeting secured with staples or by sealing the seams with a marine-grade sealant and letting it cure.

Vinyl tubs

For a larger garden, you can use a vinyl tub and construct a simple surround for it with cedar or redwood siding.

Large all-purpose tubs are available at home supply stores. Siding is often rough on one side and milled smooth on the other—you can use either side on the outside.

Once your mini-pond is ready, fill it with a pleasing arrangement of water-loving plants, such as water iris or water lilies.

Stocking Your Pond

A garden pond needs the right combination of plants, fish and snails to maintain its water clarity and ecological balance.

Aquatic plants feed and shelter fish and keep the water clear. Plant them in soil-filled containers raised to the correct height by setting them on bricks, stones or blocks set on the bottom of the pond. A pond should contain plants from all three aquatic plant groups listed below. Check each plant's growth cycle and temperature tolerance to be sure it's suited to your pond.

After you add the plants, wait at least a week before you stock the pond with fish and snails.

Submerged plants such as *Egeria* and *Cabomba* control algae, absorb fish and plant waste and release oxygen essential to fish. Use one pot (about six stems each) of plants for every 1 to 2 sq. ft. of pond surface.

Floating plants such as water lilies and water clover shade the pond's surface and keep the water cool. Their leaves should cover 60 to 70 percent of the pond surface.

Upright bog plants grow in damp soil or shallow water and add color, texture and form to a pond. They include ornamental grasses and rushes, as well as flowering plants such as water iris and pickerel rush. Use about one pot of upright plants for every 10 sq. ft. of pond surface.

Goldfish consume algae and pests such as mosquito larvae. Stock up to 1 in. of fish per 5 gal. of water—any more may make the water murky.

Black Japanese water snails eat decaying plant matter and algae off plants and pots. Add one snail for every 2 sq. ft. of pond surface.

Once you've stocked the pond, don't be alarmed if the water turns a murky green. New ponds go through a murky stage that may take four to six weeks to clear.

EASTERN INFLUENCE

This simple, elegant design is based on the lattice railing of an ancient Chinese staircase. The railing consists of 19×50-in. lattice panels assembled from redwood 1×2s. The panels are preassembled, then installed between the posts and rails with a simple dowel-and-tubing technique that makes them appear to float within the rails.

In the first step, you construct the lattice panels, following the numbered sequence shown in the illustration. In the second step, you fasten the "floating" panels to the posts and rails.

Step 1

Fasten the 1×2 lattice parts together with 2½-in. galvanized deck screws. Predrill and counterbore each screw hole ½ in. deep. Toescrew the last couple of joints, as shown. Conceal the screw heads with wood plugs or putty.

Step 2

A. Bore eight ⅜-in.-dia. holes through the perimeter frame of the lattice panel, positioned as indicated in the diagram.

B. Drill matching holes ¾ in. deep in the posts and rails.

C. Insert ⅜-in.-dia. × 3¾-in.-long

sections of hardwood dowels in the holes in the lattice panel.

D. Holding each panel in place, slip 1½-in.-long pieces of ½-in.-dia. copper tubing over each dowel.

E. To secure the panel, tap the dowels through the tubing and into the holes in the rails and posts.

Tools
- screwdriver
- hammer
- drill

Materials
- 1x2 redwood
- 2½-in. galvanized deck screws
- wood plugs or putty
- ⅜-in.-dia. hardwood dowels
- ½-in.-dia. copper tubing

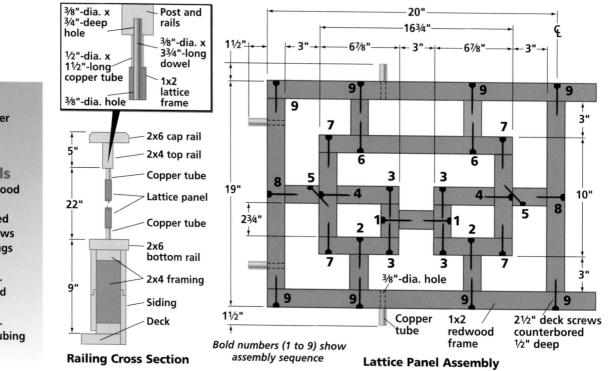

Railing Cross Section

Bold numbers (1 to 9) show assembly sequence

Lattice Panel Assembly

CEDAR LOUVERS

This louvered cedar railing has a chameleonlike visual effect that shifts with your point of view. When viewed straight on, it looks open and airy, but from any other angle the louvers block your view, creating a privacy screen. The louvers also create an everchanging play of light and shadow over the deck as the sun moves across the sky.

Deck posts are usually installed when the deck is built. If you want to bevel the tops of the posts, do this before they're set in place, using a radial arm saw (or sliding compound miter saw) with the blade set at 30 degrees.

Step 1

A. Install the 2×4 top and bottom rails between the posts.

B. Fasten 4-in. 4×4 blocks under the lower rail at midspan (or every 4 ft.) to prevent sagging.

C. Screw the hemlock handrail to the 2×4 top rails.

Step 2

A. Assemble the louver panels by nailing them in place between two horizontal 1×4s. Follow a repeating

pattern of three louvers spaced 2 in. apart, followed by a 4-in. gap.

B. Attach the assembled louver panels to the top and bottom rails

with screws (not nails), so they can be easily removed for repairs or refinishing.

Tools
- screwdriver
- hammer
- drill

Materials
- 1x4 3½-in.-wide cedar louvers
- 1x4 cedar (frame)
- 4x4 cedar (blocks)
- 2x4 cedar (rails)
- 6x6 cedar (posts)
- graspable milled-hemlock handrail (staircase banister)
- 2-in. galvanized deck screws
- #6 galvanized finishing nails

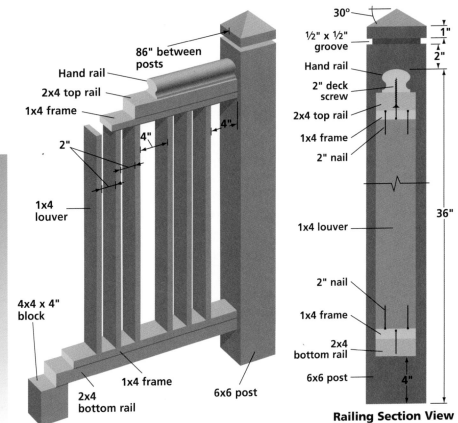

Railing Section View

TIERED PLANTERS

Multilevel planters are an attractive way to use beds of shrubs and flowering plants to separate different parts of the yard. The tiered planters shown below are built with pressure-treated 6×6 timbers that are stacked and nailed together. Start by adapting this design to your yard, then follow the construction steps shown below.

Tools
- shovel or spade
- 4-ft. level
- framing square
- drill with 11/16-in. bit
- tape measure
- sledgehammer
- circular saw

Materials
- 6x6 ground contact pressure-treated lumber
- gravel
- 10-in. landscaping spikes
- 24-in., 5/8-in.-dia. steel reinforcing bar (rebar)

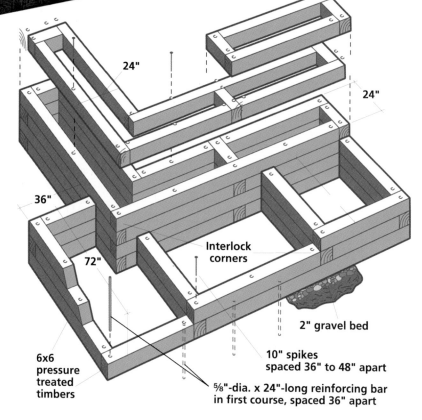

24"

24"

36"

72"

Interlock corners

2" gravel bed

6x6 pressure treated timbers

10" spikes spaced 36" to 48" apart

5/8"-dia. x 24"-long reinforcing bar in first course, spaced 36" apart

Step 1

A. Excavate a 2-in.-deep trench corresponding to the layout of the first course of timbers.

B. Pour 2 in. of gravel into the trench.

C. Compact the gravel firmly, using a spare timber to tamp it down.

Step 2

A. Lay down the first course of timbers.

B. Check to make sure the timbers are level. If necessary, add more gravel to correct any low spots or wobbles.

C. Use a framing square to set all corners at 90 degrees.

D. Bore 11/16-in.-dia. holes through the timbers, spacing the holes 3 ft. apart.

E. Insert the steel reinforcing bar pieces into the holes.

F. Use a sledgehammer to pound the reinforcing bar through the timbers and into the ground.

Step 3

Form the planters by stacking the timbers one on top of the other, interlocking them at the corners. Nail down each course as you lay it, spacing the spikes 3 to 4 ft. apart. Continue until all timbers are placed.

Step 4

A. Line the bottom of the planters with about 4 in. of gravel. Fill them up to 1 in. from the top with soil.

B. Add the plants. Spread mulch over the surface to retard weed growth and retain soil moisture.

PRIVACY SCREEN

This trio of latticed screens can create a private corner for a spa or shelter a deck. The center screen is 18 in. taller than the other two and set back to produce a tiered effect.

Tools

- posthole digger or power auger
- circular saw
- router with ¾-in. straight bit
- tape measure
- hammer
- level

Materials

- 4x4 pressure-treated pine, cedar or redwood (posts & headers)
- 4x8-ft. x 1-in. cedar lattice (3)
- 1x4 pine (temporary braces)
- 40d (6-in.) spikes (6)
- 6d & 20d galvanized nails
- ready-mix concrete
- gravel

Step 1

A. Dig six postholes (see **How to Set Posts**, page 155), placing each pair 47 in. apart.

B. Tamp 4 in. of gravel into each hole.

Step 2

A. Cut the posts and headers to length. Miter-cut the ends of the headers at 45 degrees.

B. Rout ½-in.-deep × 1-in.-wide grooves in the posts and headers. For each groove, make two passes with a ¾-in. straight bit. End them 4 in. above ground level.

Step 3

A. Slip the lattice panel into the grooves. Fit the header on top and secure it to the posts with the spikes.

B. Nail a temporary 1×4 brace across the posts near the bottom of the panel, to keep the frame square.

Step 4

A. Stand the assembled screens in the postholes and brace them upright with 1×4 lumber and stakes.

B. Make sure the posts are plumb and the headers level (if necessary, add more gravel).

C. Pour premixed concrete into the holes to just above the finished grade level. Bevel the wet concrete away from the post to allow water to run off. Let the concrete cure overnight before removing the braces.

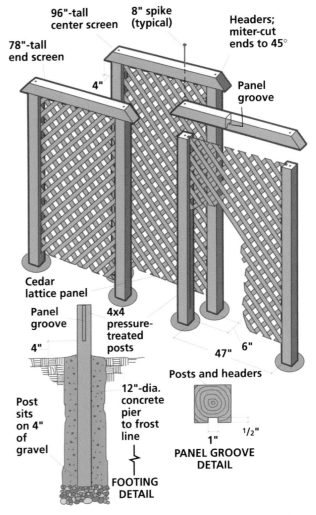

96"-tall center screen
8" spike (typical)
Headers; miter-cut ends to 45°
78"-tall end screen
4"
Panel groove
Cedar lattice panel
Panel groove
4x4 pressure-treated posts
47" 6"
Posts and headers
Post sits on 4" of gravel
4"
12"-dia. concrete pier to frost line
1" ½"
PANEL GROOVE DETAIL
FOOTING DETAIL

COZY CORNER

Tools
- circular saw
- reciprocating saw
- screwdriver
- hammer
- tape measure

Materials
- pressure-treated 4x4s
- 2x4 struts
- 1x4 trim
- ⁵⁄₄x6-in. boards
- 1-in. lattice
- 3-in. galvanized deck screws
- 6-in. x ³⁄₈-in.-dia. galvanized lag screws
- 10d (3-in.) galvanized finishing nails
- hinges and door hardware

Nestled behind this cozy corner bench are a large corner planter box and a trellis. To the left is a triangular storage cabinet that can hold barbecue utensils, serving trays and other deck accessories.

Step 1: Planter box
A. Cut pressure-treated 4×4s to the desired dimensions, mitering the front corners at 45 degrees to accommodate angled joints.

B. Construct the planter box in the corner of the deck by stacking 4×4s with overlapping corner joints. Secure the joints with deck screws.

C. Screw a vertical 2×4 strut to each of the planter's three interior walls for added support.

D. Cover the top edges with ⁵⁄₄x6-in. boards, keeping them flush with outside edges but letting them overhang on the front.

Step 2: Trellis
A. Cut two 4×4 posts to the desired height, measuring from the bottom edge of the deck. Miter the top ends as shown.

B. Secure the posts to the rear of the planter box with lag screws. The inner post should be flush with the side of the house, and the outer post with the outer corner of the planter.

C. Construct a center crossbrace from 2×4s. The vertical brace should extend 72 in. up from the top edge of the planter, with the horizontal braces placed halfway down. Double-bevel the top of the

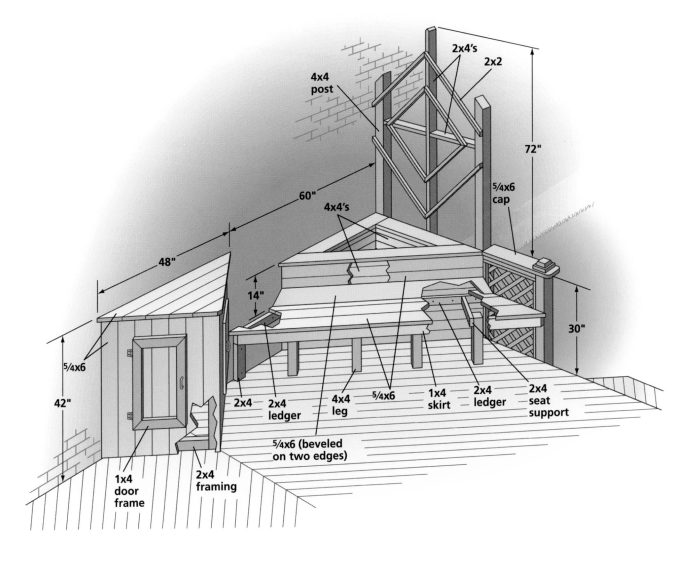

Labels in illustration:
- 2x4's
- 2x2
- 72"
- 4x4 post
- 60"
- 4x4's
- 5/4x6 cap
- 48"
- 14"
- 30"
- 5/4x6
- 42"
- 2x4
- 2x4 ledger
- 4x4 leg
- 5/4x6
- 1x4 skirt
- 2x4 ledger
- 2x4 seat support
- 5/4x6 (beveled on two edges)
- 1x4 door frame
- 2x4 framing

vertical brace. Fasten the brace between the posts with screws.

D. Cut 2×2 lattice pieces and nail them in place to create a double-diamond pattern.

Step 3: Bench seat

A. Cut a 4×4 post to extend 30 in. over the top of the deck. Secure it with lag screws to the point on the deck edge that meets the outermost corner of the bench seat.

B. Attach a 2×4 horizontal rail between this post and the outermost trellis post. Fill the space with 1-in. lattice and top the rail with a 5/4x6 cap, keeping the rail top flush with the planter top.

C. Attach four evenly spaced 2×4 seat supports to a 2×4 ledger cut to span the front of the planter. Screw the ledger to the planter 14 in. from the top edge. Screw corresponding ledgers to the house side and to the outside post.

D. Attach four 4×4 legs to the seat supports as shown, fastening a 2×4 vertical support to the house side. Fasten a 1×4 skirt to the front edge of the legs.

E. Sheath the frame in 5/4x6-in. boards, covering the bench back (planter front) as well. Place a 5/4x6 board at an angle where the seat meets the back, beveling the edges to fit.

Step 4: Storage cabinet

A. Use 2×4s to construct two 42-in.-square frames for the front of the cabinet and one 48 × 42-in. frame for the back.

B. Bevel the edges to allow for angled joints. Nail the frame together.

C. Cover the frame in 5/4x6-in. boards to match the planter and bench seat. Cut the top boards to correspond with triangular shape.

D. Cut one door opening on each front side. Use the cut-out boards to assemble each door.

E. Attach 1×4-in. frames to the front of doors. Attach hinges and door hardware.

CROSSRAIL CLASSIC

This attractive crossrail fence features a repeating crisscross pattern that's relatively easy to construct. As with any fence, the amount of time required to build it will depend largely on the length of the fence.

The components of this fence are 4×4 posts, 1×6 rails and 1×4 trim boards. The tops of the posts are protected from water damage by preformed metal post caps.

Tools
- posthole digger
- level
- hammer
- screwdriver
- plumb bob
- drill
- portable circular saw, power miter saw or radial arm saw
- paintbrush

Materials
- 4x4 pressure-treated ground contact lumber (posts)
- 1x6 pressure-treated lumber (rails)
- 1x4 pressure-treated lumber (trim)
- gravel
- 8d (2½-in.) galvanized nails
- galvanized deck screws
- metal post caps
- white 100% acrylic latex exterior paint

Step 1
A. Dig postholes, 8 ft. apart on center. Fill with 2 to 4 in. of gravel (see **How to Set Posts,** page 155).

B. Set the posts in the holes and make sure they're plumb. Backfill and compact the soil around them.

Step 2
Fasten the horizontal 1×6 rails to the posts, using 8d (2½ in.) nails. Bore pilot holes first to prevent splitting.

A. Attach the bottom rail at least 2 to 3 in. above the ground.

B. Attach the second rail from the bottom, leaving a 2¾-in. gap between the two bottom rails.

C. Attach the upper rail 4 in. down from the top of the posts.

Step 3
A. Miter-cut the ends of the 1×6 cross rails so they'll span from the center of one post to the center of the next and fit snugly between the upper and second rails.

B. Bore pilot holes. Nail the cross rails to the posts.

Step 4
A. Cut the 40-in.-long 1×4 trim.

B. Nail the trim boards to each post directly over the joints where the rails meet. (Or use galvanized deck screws, which make it easy to remove the trim boards for repair.)

Step 5
A. Attach the metal caps to the top of the posts, using the nails or screws that come with them.

B. Paint the fence.

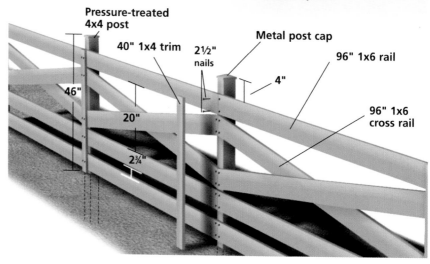

Pressure-treated 4x4 post — 40" 1x4 trim — 2½" nails — Metal post cap — 96" 1x6 rail — 96" 1x6 cross rail — 46" — 20" — 4" — 2¾"

REDWOOD SLATS

A series of closely spaced 1×4 slats gives this striking redwood fence the look of a partly open Venetian blind.

The three panels shown in the illustration measure a little over 12 ft. wide. The rails are toenailed to four 12-ft.-long 4×4 posts that protrude 8 ft. out of the ground. At one end of the screen, the fence drops down to a height of 37½ in.

Step 1

Set the four posts (see page 155) to create a 72-in.-wide center section of slats, flanked by two 36-in.-wide sections. Check that the tops are level and the same height.

Step 2

A. Toenail the horizontal 4×4 top rail to the tops of the posts.

B. Cut the 2×4 rails to fit between the posts and toenail them in place.

C. Cut all the slats to fit between the rails.

Step 3

A. Use a power miter saw or radial arm saw to cut all the angled spacer blocks from 2×4 stock. Set the saw blade to 45 degrees and cut the blocks 1½ in. wide.

Redwood deck photo courtesy of California Redwood Association

B. Bore a pilot hole through each block for an 8d (2½ in.) nail. Since the middle 2×4 rails will have spacer blocks nailed to both top and bottom surfaces, offset these pilot holes so the nails won't collide.

Step 4

A. Nail a spacer block under the top rail and another one on top of the middle rail.

B. Run a bead of construction adhesive along the sides of the blocks and install a 1×4 slat.

C. Lay another bead of construction adhesive across the surface of the slat at each end.

D. Press the next pair of blocks tightly against the slat and nail them in place.

E. Install the remaining slats in the upper tier the same way.

F. Repeat steps 4A to 4E for the lower tier of slats.

Tools
- hammer
- screwdriver
- plumb bob
- drill
- portable circular saw, power miter saw or radial arm saw

Materials
- 4x4 redwood (posts & top rails)
- 2x4 redwood (bottom & middle rails, spacer blocks)
- 1x4 redwood (slats)
- construction adhesive
- 8d (2½-in.) galvanized finishing nails

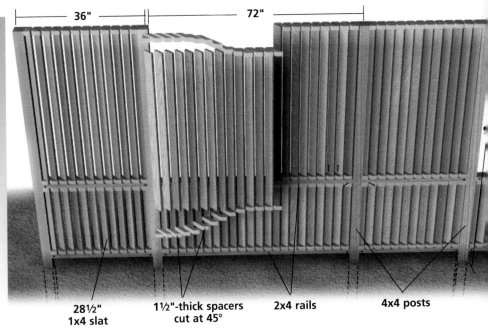

36"   72"

28½"
1x4 slat

1½"-thick spacers
cut at 45°

2x4 rails

4x4 posts

PATIO ARBOR

This impressive arbor is built entirely of construction-grade redwood, painted white for an elegant, classic look. Cedar and pressure-treated pine will also resist rot and insects, but redwood is easier to cut, less likely to warp or twist, and takes paint beautifully. We suggest painting the canopy pieces before installation to avoid having to work on an 8-ft.-high ladder.

For an experienced do-it-yourselfer, this project should take about three weekends. The first weekend, cut the lumber and apply the primer. The next weekend, paint the lumber and prepare the footings. At that point, constructing the arbor itself should take just one more day.

The arbor consists of six 7½-ft.-tall 8×8 posts topped with three pairs of 13-ft. 2-in. 2×8 beams. The beams support an overhead canopy made up of seven 17½-ft.-long 2×6 rafters and nine 10½-ft.-long 1×2 lattice strips.

Step 1

A. Cut all pieces of lumber to length.

B. Using a jigsaw, cut the ends of the beams and the rafters into an ogee profile.

C. Apply two coats of primer to all the exposed surfaces of the canopy pieces.

D. Apply two coats of paint over the primer.

Step 2

A. Lay out the footing holes for the six posts. The three rows of posts perpendicular to the house are 7 ft. 7 in. apart on center. The two rows parallel to the house are 9 ft. 6½ in. apart on center.

B. Dig each hole about 18 in. wide and 24 in. deep.

If the ground freezes in your area, you may need to dig deeper; check with your local building department for the required depth (see **How to Set Posts**, page 155).

Step 3

A. Fill each hole with concrete.

B. Before the concrete begins to set, insert a 42-in.-long piece of ¾-in.-dia. galvanized-metal pipe into the holes. Leave 18 in. of the pipe sticking straight up (perfectly plumb) in the middle.

C. Allow the concrete to cure for at least 24 hours.

Step 4

A. Using a long, 1⅛-in.-dia. auger bit, bore a center hole into the bottom end of each of the posts. Drill

at least ½ in. deeper than the protruding pipe, and be careful to keep the drill bit on a perfectly straight course. If necessary, attach the bit to an extension shaft.

B. Soak the ends of the posts in wood preservative for several hours.

C. Lift one of the posts above one of the protruding pipes; have a helper align the hole with the pipe. Slowly and carefully lower the post over the pipe until it sits on the concrete footing.

D. Repeat step 4C for the remaining five posts.

E. Check to make sure that each post is perfectly plumb.

F. If necessary, drive cedar-shingle shims beneath the posts to correct their alignment.

Tools
- posthole digger
- portable circular saw
- jigsaw
- ½-in. drill
- screwdriver
- 1⅛-in.-dia. auger bit
- hammer
- router with ¾-in. chamfering bit
- tape measure
- random-orbit sander
- paintbrush

Materials
- primer
- white acrylic latex exterior paint
- concrete
- 42-in. x ¾-in.-dia. galvanized metal pipe (outer dia.1¹⁄₁₆ in.): 6
- cedar-shingle shims
- 8x8 redwood (posts): 6
- 2x8 redwood (beams): 6
- 2x6 redwood (rafters): 7
- 1x2 redwood (lattice strips): 9
- 1x3 redwood (trim)
- ½-in.-thick pressure-treated plywood
- 3½-in. & 2½-in. galvanized deck screws
- galvanized finishing nails

Step 4

Bore a center hole into the bottom of each post, keeping the bit on a straight course.

Screw a square of pressure-treated plywood onto two 2×8s.

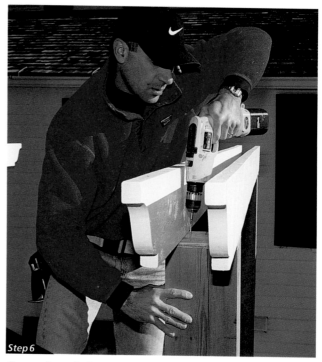

Screw through the plywood and into the top of the posts.

Prebore holes in the rafters and screw them to the beams.

Step 5

A. For each pair of double beams, cut two 7½-in.-sq. pieces of ½-in. plywood.

B. Attach the plywood plates to the bottom edge of each pair of 2×8s, using six deck screws. Position the plates to align with the posts.

Step 6

A. With a helper, raise each assembled double beam and place it on top of the posts. Carefully position the plywood plates over the posts.

B. To secure the beams, drive screws down through the plywood plates and into the tops of the posts.

Step 7

A. Lay the seven 17½-ft.-long 2×6 rafters across the beams, spacing them 20 in. on center.

B. Attach each rafter with 3½-in. decking screws driven at an angle into the 2×8s. To hold the rafter straight up on edge, place the screws alternately on one side and then the other. Drill pilot holes to prevent splitting.

Step 8

A. Lay the nine 10½-ft.-long 1×2 lattice strips across the rafters, spacing them 21½ in. on center.

B. Use a tape measure to make sure that each lattice

Position the lattice so it protrudes 2 in. over the first rafter.

Nail trim around the top of each post to suggest a capital.

strip overhangs the first rafter by 2 in. If necessary, snap lines to make sure the strips are straight.

C. Fasten the lattice strips to the rafters from above, using 2½-in. deck screws.

Step 9

Nail 1×3 trim around the top of each post. Drill pilot holes to prevent splitting.

Step 10

A. Use a router fitted with a ¾-in. chamfering bit to shape the four corner edges of each post. Start the chamfers 3 in. below the 1×3 trim and end them 20 in. above the bottom of the posts. To avoid splintering the wood or overloading the tool, make two or three progressively deeper cuts.

B. Sand the chamfers smooth, using a random-orbit sander.

C. Prime and paint the posts to match the rest of the structure.

Use a router to cut a deep chamfer into all four corners of each post before painting.

CEDAR SETTEE

This attractive red cedar settee features a pair of facing benches that remind us of an old-fashioned double glider; they provide an inviting place to relax and enjoy this backyard flower garden.

Although the settee serves here as the entrance to a garden, it could also be placed along a stone path or a wooden walkway. You could even hang a gate from it

and use it as an opening in a fence.

The structure is supported by eight 4×4 posts and measures a compact 4 × 8 ft. The overhead arbor is made of 4×4 beams topped with 2×6 joists and rafters. A decorative lattice transom tops the space below the arbor.

Tools

- posthole digger
- radial arm saw with dado blade or portable circular saw
- jigsaw
- chisel
- hammer
- clamps
- router with ¼-in.-radius roundover bit
- table saw with dado blade or router with ½-in. straight bit

Materials

- gravel
- 4×4 red cedar heartwood (posts): 8
- 4×4 red cedar (beams): 4
- 2×6 red cedar (joists & rafters): 8
- 4×8 red cedar diagonal lattice
- 2×3 red cedar (lattice frames)
- 2×4 red cedar (bench frames)
- 1×3 red cedar (bench slats)
- 1×6 red cedar (bench armrests)
- sandpaper
- 2-in. (6d) galvanized finishing nails
- 3-in. galvanized deck screws
- 3-in.-long galvanized lag screws (optional)

The bench seats consist of 2×4 frames covered with 1×3 slats. The edges of the seat slats and the contoured armrests are rounded and sanded smooth to eliminate sharp edges and to discourage splintering.

The 2×4s that support the seat are angled up 5 degrees, and those that form the seat back are angled back 10 degrees. Although these angles make your cutting job a little trickier, they provide an added level of comfort and support that you'll appreciate later.

Step 1

A. Lay out and dig eight 12-in.-dia. × 24-in.-deep postholes, as shown in the diagram. If the ground freezes in your area, you may need to dig deeper (and use longer posts). Check your local building codes for the recommended depth in your area (also see **How to Set Posts,** right).

B. Line each hole with 2 to 4 in. of compacted gravel.

Step 2

A. Cut 1¾-in.-deep × 3½-in. half-lap joints into the upper ends of eight 12-ft.-long 4×4 posts, using a radial arm saw fitted with a dado blade. Set the blade depth to 1¾ in. and cut a series of closely spaced kerfs. (You can also cut these joints with a portable circular saw.)

To save time, clamp the posts and beams together and cut several lap joints at the same time.

B. Cut matching half-laps in the four 4×4 horizontal beams.

C. Join the beams to the posts with 3-in. deck screws.

Step 3

A. Set the post/beam assemblies into the holes.

B. Brace them plumb, backfill with dirt and compact well (or use concrete). The posts should protrude from the holes 10 ft. 2 in.

Step 4

A. Using a jigsaw, cut the decorative profile onto the ends of the four 10-ft.-long 2×6 joists.

B. Toescrew the joists to the beams with 3-in. screws.

If you wish, you can secure the first and last joists to the posts with 3-in.-long deck or lag screws.

Step 5

A. Cut and assemble the four rafters from 2×6 stock.

B. Fasten the rafters to the joists, using 3-in. screws.

HOW TO SET POSTS

Most fence and gate projects begin with digging postholes. The posts are typically spaced 6 to 8 ft. apart, depending on the design of the fence. Check your local Building Codes for the required setback from buildings and property lines. Also check the required posthole depth, which will depend on the frost line in your area. The diameter of a posthole should usually be 12 in. or more, or about 3 times wider than the post.

1. Dig the holes with a shovel, posthole digger or rented power auger. If you have many holes to dig, use a power auger.

2. Line the holes with 2 to 4 in. of gravel to ensure good drainage.

3. Set the posts in the holes and tamp down the dirt all around.

4. Posts that support a gate or that stand at the end of a fence require concrete footings: Dig the hole below the frost line and add 4 in. of gravel. Set the post in the hole, brace it and fill the hole with concrete. Allow to dry overnight.

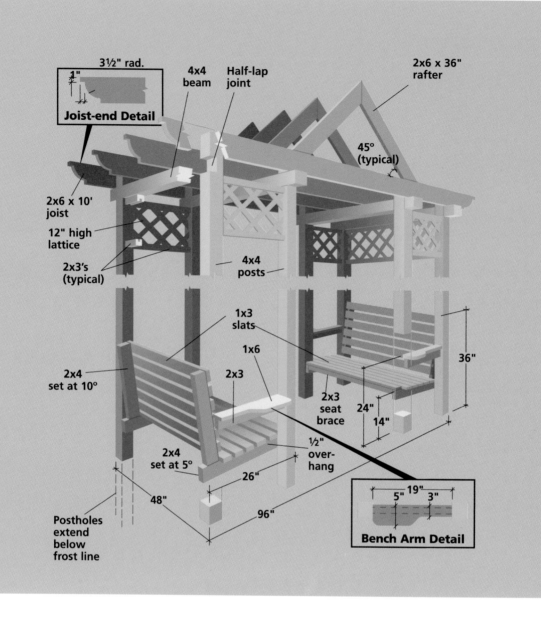

3½" rad.
1"
Joist-end Detail

4x4 beam
Half-lap joint

2x6 x 36" rafter

45° (typical)

2x6 x 10' joist

12" high lattice

2x3's (typical)

4x4 posts

1x3 slats

1x6

2x4 set at 10°

2x3

36"

2x3 seat brace

24"

14"

½" over-hang

2x4 set at 5°

26"

48"

96"

Postholes extend below frost line

19"
5" 3"
Bench Arm Detail

Step 6

A. Cut to length the diagonal lattice and the 2×3 frames for the lattice transom panels.

B. Make ½×½-in. grooves on the inside of the frame pieces, using a dado blade on a table saw, or a router fitted with a ½-in. straight or mortising bit.

C. Fasten the transom panels in place with 3-in. screws.

Step 7

Fasten the 2×3 and 2×4 bench frame parts to the posts, using 3-in. screws.

Step 8

A. Cut to length all the 1×3 slats for the seat and the back.

B. Shape the edges with a router and ¼-in.-radius roundover bit. Sand until smooth.

C. Secure the slats with 2-in. nails.

Step 9

A. Use a jigsaw to cut the bench arms from 1×6 stock.

B. Shape the edges with a router and ¼-in.-radius roundover bit. Sand until smooth.

C. Secure the bench arms with 2-in. nails.

Index

A
Adobe pattern, 9
Arbors, 133
  cedar settee, 154-156
  patio, 150-153
Architectural millwork, 91
Asphalt-based mastic, 22
Automatic switches, 65

B
Backsplash, 27
Bathtubs, 51
  glass tub enclosure, 56-57
  solid-surface tub surround, 58-59
Batting, 14
Beadboard ceiling, 46-47
Benches, 146-147, 154-156
Beveling, 146-147
Bifold closet doors, 98-99
Bin and shelving units, 106-107
Bookcases, 103
  floor-to-ceiling, 122-125
  wall-to-wall, 116-117
Borders,
  how to miter corners, 13
  wallpaper, 12-13
Brocade design, 9
Buckling, preventing, 86
Building codes, 155

C
Cabinets, 116-117, 118-121
  choosing, 117
Casement windows, 71
Ceiling fan-light, 68-69
Ceilings, 31
  beadboard, 46-47
  embossed tin, 45
  layered, 42-43
  textured, 44
Ceramic tile,
  flooring, 32-33
Chair rail molding, 20
Closet doors, 98-99
Compound-angle miter joint, 18
Compression strips, rubber, 86
Crown molding, 18-19, 47, 104-105,
  116, 121
Crowsfoot design, 9
Curing, 33, 40, 55, 135, 151

D
Decks, 133
  add-ons, 144-147
  railings, 142-143
Decorative painting, 10-11
Dentil molding, 105
Dimmer switches, 64
Display shelving, 103
  bin-and-shelving units, 106-107
  mantel shelf, 104-105
  wall boxes, 108-109
Door sweep, 87, 95
Doors, 85
  closet, 98-99
  garage, 87
  grand entrance, 90-93
  screen, 96-97
  securing, 89
  security locks and, 88
  storm, 94-95
  weatherizing, 86-87
Double-hung windows, 70-71
Drafts, 86, 89
Dry-back tile, 34-35
Drywall, 43, 44, 113

E
Electrical box, 68-69
Embossed tin ceiling, 45
Entertainment center, 118-121
  glide-out shelves, 118, 128-129
Entries, 85

F
Fabric, 14-15
  worksheet, 15
Face-nailing, 47
Fan pattern, 44
Fasteners,
  using, 22-23
Fences, 133
  crossrail classic, 148
  redwood slats, 149
Fin, flexible rubber, 93
Flooring, 31
  ceramic tile, 32-33
  laminate, 38-41
  sheet vinyl, 36-37
  vinyl tile, 34-35
Floor roller, 37
Fluorescent fixtures, 127
Framing square, 144
Full-spread vinyl, 36-37

G
Garage doors, 87
Gates, 133
  cedar, 154-156
Glass block window, 76-79
Glass ceiling, 24
Glass tub enclosure, 56-57
Glide-out shelves, 128-129
Gloves, 20
Grand entrance, 90-93
Grommet plates, 127

H
Halogen light fixtures, 26, 27, 126, 127
Heavy-nap roller, 9, 44, 45

I
Incandescent lights, 126

J
Jamb brackets, 99
J-bead, 43
J-channel, 27
J-roller, 37, 59

K
Kitchen wine rack, 112-113
Knockdown pattern, 44

L
Laminate flooring, 38-41
  layers, 39
Latticed screens, 142, 145
Layered ceiling, 42-43
Library panels, 21
Lighting, 63
  ceiling fan, 68-69
  dimmer switches, 64
  recessed, 66-67
  specialty switches, 65
  a wall unit, 126-127
Linoleum knife, 37
Locks, security, 88

M
Mantel shelf, 104-105
Marbling, 11
Mastic, 24, 25, 26, 27, 55
  using, 22-23
Miniature light systems, 127
Mini-tracks, 127
Mirrors, 7
  backsplash, 27
  bath ideas, 24-26

buying, 23
cleaning, 25
designing with, 22-23
mounting, 23
Molding,
  crown, 18-19, 47, 104-105, 116, 121
  dentil, 105
  wall frame, 16-17
Mortar, 55, 140
Motion-sensing switches, 65

N
Neon circuit tester, 64, 67, 68

O
Orange-peel texture, 44

P
Painting, 17, 19, 43, 45, 47, 75, 105, 107,
  109, 113, 115, 148, 151
  decorative, 10-11
  texture, 8-9
Pantry, stairway, 114-115
Patio arbor, 150-153
Perimeter-bond vinyl, 36-37
Picture frame shelves, 110-111
Planters, 140, 144-145
Plumb, checking for, 53, 56-57, 91, 111,
  124, 145, 148, 151
Pneumatic door closer, 97
Polychrome ceiling, 45
Polyethylene vapor barrier, 41
Postholes, 148, 149, 151
  setting, 155
Pressed-metal wainscoting, 20
Programmable switches, 65
Puck lights, 127

Q
Quick-setting mastic, 23

R
Railings, deck,
  cedar louvers, 143
  eastern influence, 142
Recessed lighting, 66-67
Recessed shelving, 103
  pantry, 114-115
  picture frame shelves, 110-111
  wine rack, 112-113
Respirator, 58
Rubber sweep, 87
Rusting, protection against, 20

S
Sand float texture, 44
Sanding, 75, 105, 107, 115, 125, 129
Sashes, replacing, 72-73
Scoring, 33, 43
Screen doors, 96-97
Screen, privacy, 145
Security locks, 88
Self-adhesive compressible foam, 71
Self-adhesive tile, 34-35
Settee, 154-156
Sheet vinyl flooring, 36-37
Shelving,
  add-ons, 103, 126-129
  display, 103, 104-109
  recessed, 103, 110-115
  wall units, 103, 116-125
Showerheads, slide-bar, 53
Showers, 51
  porcelain soap dish, 52
  seat, 54-55
  slide-bar showerhead, 53
Shutters, interior, 74-75
Skip-trowel finish, 44
Skylights, 63
  tubular, 80-81
Sleeves, metal, 89
Slide-bar showerhead, 53
Sliding windows, 71
Soap dish, porcelain, 52
Solid-surface tub surround, 58-59
Specialty switches, 65
Splattered finish, 44
Spline roller, 97
Splintering, discouraging, 155
Splitting, preventing, 47, 148
Sponge, 9, 10-11, 13, 33, 55
Sponging, 10-11
Stairway pantry, 114-115
Stipple texture, 9
Stomp design, 9
Storage cabinet, 146. *See also* Shelving
Storm doors, 94-95
Storm windows, 71
Strip lighting, 127
Stucco pattern, 9
Swirl pattern, 9, 44

T
Tamping, 144, 145, 155
Teflon tape, 53
Texture painting, 8-9
  ceilings, 44
  suggestions, 9

Tile adhesive, 33
Tin ceiling, 45
Tin snips, 20
Toenailing, 120, 149
Toescrewing, 118, 134, 142, 155
Tools and materials,
  bathtubs, 56, 58
  ceilings, 42, 44, 45, 46
  decks, 142, 143, 144, 145, 146
  doors, 86, 88, 89, 90, 94, 96, 98
  fences, 148, 149
  floors, 32, 34, 36, 38
  gates and arbors, 150, 154
  lighting, 64, 66, 68, 126
  mirrors, 22, 24, 26, 27
  shelves, 104, 106, 108, 110, 112, 114,
    116, 118, 122, 126, 128
  showers, 52, 53, 54
  wainscots, 20, 21
  wall treatments, 8, 10, 12, 14, 16, 18
  wall units, 116, 118, 122
  windows, 70, 72, 74, 76
Track lighting, 126
  trouble shooting, 127
Trellis, 146-147
Trowel, 9, 44, 55
Tubs, 51
  glass tub enclosure, 56-57
  solid-surface tub surround, 58-59
Tubular skylight, 80-81
Two-tone stucco, 9

U
Underlayment, 41
Upholstered walls, 14-15
Urethane adhesive, 92-93
Urethane molding styles, 18-19

V
Varnish, 21, 45
V-channel weatherstripping, 70-71, 86
Veining, 11
Veneer plaster, 44
Vent screens, 126
Vinyl tile,
  flooring, 34-35

W
Wainscoting, 7
  library panels, 21
  pressed-metal, 20
Wall boxes, 108-109
Wall frame molding, 16-17
Wallpaper borders, 12-13

Photography Credits

Wall treatments, 7
  crown molding, 18-19
  decorative painting, 10-11
  texture painting, 8-9
  uphostered walls, 14-15
  wall frame molding, 16-17
  wallpaper borders, 12-13
Wall trim, 7
Wall units, 103
  bookcases, 116-117, 122-125
  entertainment center, 118-121
  floor-to-ceiling shelves, 122-125
Weatherizing,
  doors, 86-87
  windows, 70-71
Weatherproof glue, 96
Welting, double, 14-15
Wide-angle viewer, 87
Windows, 63
  glass block, 76-77
  replacing sashes, 72-73
  shutters, interior, 74-75
  skylights, 80-81
  weatherizing, 70-71
Wine rack, 112-113
Wire connection box, 67
Wire organizers, 126-127

Y
Yard improvements, 133

Creative Publishing international, Inc.
offers a variety of how-to books.
For information write:
  Creative Publishing international, Inc.
  Subscriber Books
  5900 Green Oak Drive
  Minnetonka, MN 55343

(Note: T=Top, C=Center, B=Bottom,
  L=Left, R=Right, I=Inset)

Stephen Alvarez
Sewanee, TN
© Stephen Alvarez: p. 146

Carolyn Bates
© Carolyn Bates: p. 7

Alderman Studios
High Point, NC
© Alderman Studios: pp. 118 both,
  120-121 all

Woody Cady
Bethesda, MD
© Woody Cady: pp. 25T, 144, 145, 148

Crandall & Crandall
Dana Point, CA
© Crandall & Crandall: p. 133

Stephen Cridland
Portland, OR
© Stephen Cridland: cover TL, p. 26

Chris Eden
Seattle, WA
© Chris Eden / Eden Arts: pp. 42, 43B

Derek Fell
Gardenville, PA
© Derek Fell: pp. 138-140 all

Bob Firth
Minnetonka, MN
© Bob Firth: p. 99 both

Merle Henkenius
Lincoln, NE
© Merle Henkenius: pp. 54-55 all

Roy Inman Photography
Lenexa, KS
© Roy Inman Photography: pp. 32-33 all,
  46-47 all, 72-73 all, 76-79 all

Thomas H. Jones
King of Prussia, PA
© Thomas H. Jones: pp. 20-21 all

Jeff Krueger Photography
St. Paul, MN
© Jeff Krueger Photography: p. 98

Smith-Baer Photography
Port Chester, NY
© Smith-Baer Photography: cover TR,
  cover BR, cover C, pp. 18, 19 all, 51,

56-57 all, 52-53 all, 63T, 68-69 all, 74-75
  all, 90-93 all, 96-97 all, 112-113 all,
  128-129 all, 150-153 all

Charles Mann
Santa Fe, NM
© Charles Mann: p. 141B

Lisa Masson
Arlington, VA
© Lisa Masson: p. 6

Karen Melvin
Keith Waters & Associates, Inc., Architect
Minneapolis, MN
© Karen Melvin: pp. 3B, 28-29

Melabee M. Miller
Hillside, NJ
© Melabee M. Miller: pp. 3E, 22, 62, 82-83

John Nasta
Charlotte, NC
© John Nasta: pp. 3A, 4-5, 103BL, 114

Tom Rider Architectural Photography
Petaluma, CA
© Tom Rider: p. 142

Jerry Pavia
Bonners Ferry, ID
© Jerry Pavia: p. 134

Robert Perron / Steve Lasar, Architect
Branford, CT
© Robert Perron: p. 63B

Keith Talley
Temple, TX
© Keith Talley: p. 58-59 all

Michael S. Thompson
Eugene, OR
© Michael S. Thompson: pp. 3G, 130-131,
  133T

Jessie Walker
Glencoe, IL
© Jessie Walker: pp. 23, 102

Wil Zehr / Residential Construction
  Consultants
Champaign, IL
© Wil Zehr Photography: p. 81 all

Tim Proctor & Associates, Inc. /
  Mannington Resilient Floors
Burlington, NJ
© Tim Proctor: pp. 30, 31, 34T, 36, 38

Illustration Credits

© Andrew Christie: p. 99TR

© Creative Publishing international, Inc.
(John T. Drigot): p. 105

© Creative Publishing international, Inc.
(Richard Stromwell): pp. 26B, 27B, 45B,
97B, 119, 123

© Arlo Faber: p. 115, 148B, 149B

© Mario Ferro: pp. 20B, 21B, 117, 147

© Greg Mason: p. 39TR

© Tom Moore: p. 80

© Paul Perreault and Trevor Johnston:
p. 43T

© Eugene Thompson: pp. 142B, 143B, 156

© Today's Homeowner: pp. 144B, 145B

© Andrew Van Dis: p. 27T

© Ian Worpole: pp. 24B, 25B

Contributors

Armstrong World Industries: p. 39TL
2500 Columbia Avenue, #5B
Lancaster, PA 17603
tel: 888-ARM-STRONG
http://www.armstrongfloors.com

California Redwood Association:
back cover, pp. 132, 149
405 Enfrente Drive, Suite 200
Novato, CA 94949
tel: 415-382-0662
fax: 415-382-8531
http://www.calredwood.org

Cole Sewell Corporation: p. 94
2288 University Avenue
St. Paul, MN 55114
tel: 651-605-4600
fax: 651-605-4650

Crossville Ceramics: pp. 3C, 48-49, 50
P. O. Box 1168
Crossville, TN 38557
tel: 931-484-2110
fax: 931-456-3993
http://www.crossville-ceramics.com

Bruce Laminate Floors: p. 41B
16803 Dallas Parkway
Addison, TX 75001
tel: 214-887-2100
fax: 214-887-2234
http://www.brucelaminatefloors.com

Four Seasons Solar Products Corp.:
pp. 3D, 60-61
5005 Veterans Memorial Hwy.
Holbrook, NY 11741
tel: 800-FOUR SEASONS
fax: 516-563-4010
http://www.four-seasons-sunrooms.com

Lilypons Water Gardens: p. 141T
P. O. Box 10
Buckeystown, MD 21717-0010
tel: 301-874-5503
fax: 301-874-2959
http://www.lilypons.com

Mannington Resilient Floors:
pp. 30, 31, 34T, 36, 38
P. O. Box 30
Salem, NJ 08079-0030
tel: 609-935-3000
fax: 609-339-5948

Robern, Inc.: p. 28
701 North Wilson Ave.
Bristol, PA 19007
tel: 215-826-9800
fax: 215-826-9633
http://www.robern.com

Shanker Industries, Inc.: p. 45T
3435 Lawson Boulevard
Oceanside, NY 11572
tel: 516-766-4477
fax: 516-766-6655

Simpson Door Company: p. 85
400 Simpson Avenue
McCleary, WA 98557
tel: 800-952-4057
fax: 360-495-3295
http://www.simpsondoor.com

The Stanley Works: p. 84
1000 Stanley Drive
New Britain, CT 06053
tel: 800-STANLEY
fax: 860-827-3910
http://www.stanleyworks.com

The Toro Company: p. 136
8111 Lyndale Avenue South
Bloomington, MN 55420-1196
tel: 800-595-6841
fax: 612-887-7929
http://www.toro.com

USG Corporation: p. 44 both
125 So. Franklin Street
Chicago, IL 60606
tel: 312-606-4122
fax: 312-606-5301
http://www.usg.com

Ventana USA: back cover T
6001 Enterprise Drive
Export, PA 15632
tel: 724-325-3400
fax: 724-327-4540

Wall Magic by Wagner Spray Tech Corp.:
p.10T
1770 Fernbroook Lane
Plymouth, MN 55447
tel: 800-328-8251
fax: 612-509-7555
http://www.wagnerspraytech.com

Western Red Cedar Lumber Association:
pp. 143, 154
1200-555 Burrard Street
Vancouver, British Columbia
Canada V7X 1S7
tel: 604-684-0255
fax: 604-687-4930
http://www.wrcla.org

Wood-Mode Inc.: pp. 3F, 100-101, 116
One Second Street
Kreamer, PA 17833
tel: 570-374-2711
fax: 570-372-1422
http://www.wood-mode.com